Praise for *The Unexpected Leader*

"For seasoned, aspiring, and even the most reluctant leaders, *The Unexpected Leader* is the timely and relevant leadership guide you didn't know you needed. Redefining what – and where – it means to be a leader, Jacqueline shares candid, practical insights to identify, sharpen, and elevate the leader inside of you. Whether leading within an organization, your family, social circle, or community, *The Unexpected Leader* is your definitive, actionable blueprint to embracing and cultivating the leader within and empowering others to do the same."

—Reneé Fluker,
Founder and President, The Midnight Golf Program

"*The Unexpected Leader* provides a unique perspective on what it means to be a leader, whether at work, at home, or in the community, and provides a compelling case for why we are all everyday leaders in life. Jacqueline M. Baker masterfully outlines how each of us can strengthen our leadership skills through tools, frameworks, and real-life examples. In an increasingly complex world, *The Unexpected Leader* is what we need now more than ever."

—Andy Miller,
Senior Vice President, AARP Innovation Labs

"'For our own success to be real, it must contribute to the success of others.' This quote by Eleanor Roosevelt shares Jacqueline M. Baker's passion in her book *The Unexpected Leader: Discovering the Leader Within You*. Her book inspires leadership development at all levels and helps us understand our own personal role in our leadership journey. From what to expect when making a leadership decision to knowing the pitfalls of self-sabotage, you will enjoy learning from Jacqueline's shared experiences and approach to leadership success."

—Pamela Eyring,
President, The Protocol School of Washington

"Jacqueline Baker does it again in her new book, *The Unexpected Leader,* by challenging readers in their thinking about leadership. She has you pondering on your own leadership journey and tells her readers that you must take responsibility for elevating your own leadership journey. She provides helpful tips for success (i.e., make sure you make time to invest in your leadership) and pitfalls to avoid that could derail your success (i.e., don't self-sabotage). It's a fascinating read and will inspire you to level up your own leadership."

—Tonya Berry,
Senior Vice President of Transformation & Engineering, Consumers Energy

"There are countless books that celebrate leadership in the business world. What I love about *The Unexpected Leader* is that it is designed to empower leaders at work and in our communities, who make the world a better place without fanfare. *The Unexpected Leader* uplifts those leaders, gives them permission to own their leadership, and provides tangible tools and frameworks to help strengthen their skills. As the boundaries blur between our work and home lives, we need guidance on how to be our very best selves no matter the context. *The Unexpected Leader* is that guide."

—Dr. Marlo Rencher,
Founder, Tech Founder Academy; Co-founder, Commune Angels

"At a time when professionals are leaving the workforce in record numbers, people are desperately searching for real meaning and motivation in their lives. *The Unexpected Leader* is a true roadmap to powerful self-exploration, both personally and professionally.

Whether it's finding your voice, leveraging your tribe, or avoiding pitfalls we all make, Jacqueline Baker offers realistic, tangible advice and examples that tap into the leadership potential we all possess."

—Jocelyn K. Coley,
Co-founder and CEO, The Allen Lewis Agency

the unexpected leader

DISCOVERING THE LEADER WITHIN YOU

jacqueline m. baker

FOREWORD BY **JACQUELINE M. WELCH**
EXECUTIVE VICE PRESIDENT, *THE NEW YORK TIMES*

WILEY

Published by John Wiley & Sons, Inc., Hoboken, New Jersey.
Published simultaneously in Canada.

For general information on our other products and services or for technical support, please contact our Customer Care Department within the United States at (800) 762-2974, outside the United States at (317) 572-3993 or fax (317) 572-4002.

Wiley publishes in a variety of print and electronic formats and by print-on-demand. Some material included with standard print versions of this book may not be included in e-books or in print-on-demand. If this book refers to media such as a CD or DVD that is not included in the version you purchased, you may download this material at http://booksupport.wiley.com. For more information about Wiley products, visit www.wiley.com.

Library of Congress Cataloging-in-Publication Data
Names: Baker, Jacqueline M., author.
Title: The Unexpected Leader : Discovering the Leader Within You / Jacqueline M. Baker.
Description: Hoboken, New Jersey : John Wiley & Sons, 2022. | Includes index.
Identifiers: LCCN 2022019984 (print) | LCCN 2022019985 (ebook) | ISBN 9781119877677 (cloth) | ISBN 9781119877691 (adobe pdf) | ISBN 9781119877684 (epub)
Subjects: LCSH: Leadership. | Women executives.
Classification: LCC HD57.7 .B345 2022 (print) | LCC HD57.7 (ebook) | DDC 658.4/092—dc23/eng/20220603
LC record available at https://lccn.loc.gov/2022019984
LC ebook record available at https://lccn.loc.gov/2022019985

Cover Design: Paul McCarthy

SKY10035308_071522

Just Start™

CONTENTS

FOREWORD

I Googled "leadership books," and got back 3,070,000,000 hits. This, in a word, is dizzying. Nevertheless, I stuck with the search to gain insight on this extensively covered yet hard to define topic. Some of the books purport to define leadership definitively. Others provide very specific formulas that—so the promise goes—if we faithfully employ them will turn us all into world-class leaders. All are written well enough to be in print and, I am happy to believe, all were written in good faith. In my scan, few if any even remotely attempt to address leadership in the way that Jacqueline M. Baker does in *The Unexpected Leader*.

Ms. Baker brings to the topic of leadership a broad base of experience, including instructional design, business development inside of corporations and nonprofits, entrepreneurship, and for-profit board service. While growing as a leader herself, she has simultaneously witnessed leadership as demonstrated by many others. This book is a thoughtfully curated composite of those experiences. We are given great examples and strong warnings with direct and immediate application. Best of all, as you read *The Unexpected Leader,* you feel Ms. Baker's personal relish for the topic and her genuine desire to help you elevate your own leadership skills in every area of your life.

I am a human resource professional. People are my "business." I make this characterization of Ms. Baker's work based on three decades (and counting) of watching the best and worst of leadership on display in domestic and international enterprises behemoth and small, across industries and geographies and as lived out by people of every imaginable composite sketch and demographic profile. Beyond my day job I've seen all manner of attempts at leadership as an athlete, as a nonprofit volunteer, and as a PTA mom. I've made my own attempts at being a leader across many aspects of my own life.

Based on my own lived experiences and visibility to that of countless others, here are a couple of things Ms. Baker does differently in her must-read book:

She employs an anthropological approach to finding examples of leadership in everyday life—at work, at home, and during leisure. By so elegantly opening the aperture of where we might find leadership, she subtly gives each of us a way to see ourselves as leaders. With that inhibition taken down, we read the book with a spirit of curiosity—how is this applicable to my life?

She takes into account the many ways in which the world is in a constant state of change. As one example, in the workplace we are shifting our focus away from traditional degrees and more onto skills, increasing the likelihood that we have staff and teams with high technical and functional skills but thinner relational skills. At home, the definition of family continues to broaden to include multigenerational households and gender fluidity. Who leads in the home could be younger, older, or gender unspecified.

This book challenges the idea that we rise to occasion and replaces it with the reality that we rise to our level of training. Throughout the book, Ms. Baker provides a plethora of concrete examples of leadership in action in both conventional and unconventional settings, cementing that leadership is on display even in the most unlikely of places and through sometimes the least suspecting people. Leadership then is not a place on an organizational chart, but rather a state of being, a way of showing up in the world ready to contribute, to serve, to impact what happens and how it happens.

The Unexpected Leader is a good read. It is an important read. And it is a read for everyone and anyone who wants to define and elevate a style of leadership specific to them and their ambitions.

Jacqueline M. Welch
Executive Vice President, Chief Human Resources Officer
New York Times

ACKNOWLEDGMENTS

I understand the power of community and I accept the responsibility of both receiving and giving.

And because of that, I must give thanks and acknowledgment to these wonderful people who are a bright light, amazing humans, leaders in their own lane and responsible for helping this book come to life.

First, I need to say thanks to every friend, family member, and silent supporter who has sent well wishes and kind words, and provided input throughout the process of writing this book. There isn't enough ink and paper to thank you all. I take great pride in expressing my gratitude to you directly every chance that I get.

Marc Baker: What an amazing way to spend this life—with you. The world needs more humans like you, buddy.

Andrea Williams: For your brilliant design mind and contribution of the images throughout this book and for being a great friend.

Amber Cabral: For opening doors, opening minds, and being a warm, bright yellow light that the world needs more of.

Jacqueline M. Welch: For challenging norms, challenging me, and being human, although we all know you're full of superpowers.

Jessica Hayes: For being a leader in your own lane and a role model for entrepreneurial leaders, and for your contributions to this book.

Julie Kerr: For your way with words and your editorial accountability.

Derrick and Rajoielle Register: For being the quiet but impactful supporters you always are.

Tyneshia E. McCray: For keeping all of the trains, planes and automobiles of our leadership journey on track.

INTRODUCTION

Surprise!

Think about the last time that you were legitimately surprised, in a *good* way. Reflect on where you were, who you were with, and—most important—how it made you feel.

Those eight little letters, s-u-r-p-r-i-s-e, have the ability to delight, amaze, astonish, and positively shock you.

If I reflect on my own *good* surprise from the past, my mind immediately wanders back to a surprise birthday party that was thrown for me, which was actually a double surprise because my husband proposed to me that evening as well. It was surely a magical night that will never be forgotten.

Now, as someone who spent a significant number of years as a wedding and event producer, I know that surprises can be both awesome and slightly cringeworthy. Because I am a detail-oriented kind of person, I get deeply immersed in the particulars, and when I don't know what's going on, it sends me into a wormhole of "what-ifs."

And while, over the years, I have escaped some of that "always need to know" and be involved in all of the details, the truth is that many surprises have the potential of being less of a surprise and creep more into the realm of the unexpected.

The Unexpected

Although the words "surprise" and "unexpected" live in the same realm, they have some differences.

The unexpected can surface discomfort, confusion, and frustration—and understandably so. Dealing with the unexpected can send you in a tailspin of emotion that can be, well, unexpected.

The following phrases probably evoke some level of discomfort for you, in this very moment:

- "I just didn't see that coming."
- "It was so unexpected."
- "That caught me off guard."
- "If I had expected that, then . . ."
- "If someone had just set some expectations, then . . ."

But, so many words, including the word "unexpected," can evoke both negative *and* positive feelings, just like the word "surprise."

Think about the last time that you:

- Found warm folded money as you unloaded your dryer
- Made a purchase that was significantly less than what you anticipated
- Stepped on the scale and saw a number far beneath what you expected
- Watched a movie that ended up being good rather than another wasted 156 minutes of your life
- Completed yet another video call that was 25 minutes instead of the allotted 60 minutes

These unexpected outcomes were likely very much appreciated. So, while setting expectations is an option and is welcomed in our lives, embracing the unexpected can have an equal (or even stronger) positive impact as well.

So, what else? What are the areas in our lives where embracing the unexpected can deliver value and impact?

How about *leadership?*

Leadership can often be categorized as an elusive concept that is impenetrable and unreachable. It often has this coveted air about it that seems almost mystical. While some of this cloak-and-daggering that happens when we talk about leadership has begun to unravel as the world embraces more leaders of different backgrounds and experiences, there is still much more work to be done in this area.

With the various benefits of embracing leadership that exist, there are still billions of people across the world who do not see themselves as leaders. They are unaware that at any level—regardless of whether they have acquired a top-tier salary, a corner office, a fancy car, the finest tailored suits, an army of direct reports, or an Ivy League or HBCU degree—they too have the ability to welcome the benefits and opportunities that come along with embracing the title of leadership.

Let me take a moment and address the very real elephant in the room for a moment.

Yes, there are people who probably have had the banner of *leader* over their heads since the moment that they took their first steps, ascended to varsity volleyball as a freshman, made the honor roll every year since preschool, served as debate team captain from undergraduate through graduate school, became the youngest person to make partner at their firm, won a marathon before the age of 20, and a host of other accomplishments. And, while these are not minor accomplishments, this is not the path of so many people navigating their way through their personal and professional lives.

So does this mean that only the very visible, super-accomplished, scholarly people of the world can be designated as leaders? Does this mean if you've chosen or organically happen to be a "quiet storm" or have broken out of your shell later in life, that, unbeknownst to you, you've signed up for a life without the leader title, forever?

Well, that just can't be. . . .

If we think about some of the most groundbreaking accomplishments and innovations, they've been pioneered by individuals who've led a life less out front and visible. This abbreviated list of individuals should help paint the picture for you:

Larry Page was the co-founder of Google and CEO of Alphabet. His appointment to the position was seen as odd because he is highly reserved, and even referred to as "geeky." The reality is that his quiet, intellectual nature allowed him to create an innovative new product and cultivate a unique brand that is a part of many people's everyday lives.

Albert Einstein, who most of us know as one of the most famous scientists in history, had another not so well-known trait. He was an introvert. He believed that his creativity and success came from keeping to himself and that monotony and the solitude of a quiet life stimulates the creative mind.

Marissa Mayer, former CEO at Yahoo, co-founded tech incubator Lumi Labs. She doesn't much care for crowds or parties either. She admits to being a proud introvert.

Theodor Geisel, better known as Dr. Seuss, was a quiet man who rarely ventured from his seaside home in La Jolla, California.

Steve Wozniak, Apple co-founder, came up with a world- and life-changing idea that we've all grown to know and love, then he leveraged the very visible and extroverted nature of Steve Jobs to execute his idea and bring it to scale. Introverted leaders can sit alone in quiet rooms and change the landscape of technology as we know it.

Rosa Parks's bold and courageous move was to refuse to give up her seat to a white passenger onboard a bus in Montgomery, Alabama, in the 1950s.

These people are certainly well-known, celebrated, and have either created or benefited from a legacy built for them well beyond their death in many cases. But they weren't part of an attention-seeking mainstream; they left an undeniable legacy without seeking out the spotlight that is often unnecessarily tied to the idea of leadership.

Furthermore, when we think about leadership, we have to advance past the notion that only the high achievers, massive goal setters, and members of the "winner's" circle are leaders. Let me ask you something for you to reflect on. Whether it was grade school, middle school, or high school, who were your class clowns? You know—the people who were mischievous, slightly (or very) naughty, or who just couldn't keep themselves out of the principal's office?

Or better yet, think of some of the most notorious and ruthless criminals and mob bosses of the last hundred years. While the activities these people engage in may not necessarily resonate with how we choose to live our lives, these people also possess leadership skills. They were influential, they were marching toward an individual or group goal, and they were also likely great delegators.

As for the class clowns, they too possess leadership qualities, because more often than not they had other people in your classes on board for their shenanigans, mischievous activities, and sometimes insubordinate behavior. And, let's also be honest, most of us remember who those class clowns were. They were memorable, which is also a leadership quality.

Now, I'm not encouraging you to use your leadership skills to indulge in bad behavior, but I want you to recognize that your ability to embrace and *positively* elevate your leadership skills is reasonable, within reach, and fully attainable.

Your leadership journey does not need to be a carbon copy of anyone else's. You don't have to win the highest honors or be the most popular person in any of the spaces that you show up in in order to be designated as a leader or—more importantly—to grow into a better leader.

When I reflect on my own personal journey, I immediately think of the word "invisible." As I'll share with you throughout the book, I've had what has felt like a rocky, nonlinear path in my earlier life.

As I venture back to my early teenage years, I think about how invisible I felt from the very beginning. First of all, my aunt raised me from age 12 onward and I moved with her as I was transitioning from middle school to high school. While I am always quick to say that I am ultra-grateful to my aunt for taking care of me at a time where the feeling of abandonment from my own parents was at an ultimate high, I still couldn't ever shake this feeling of being an extra kid.

Looking back at those hugely impactful years, even with my internal abandonment feelings and any family challenges, I honestly wouldn't change a thing. The outcome of that experience is that I have what are really two *bonus* siblings, because my cousins Derrick and Samantha (my aunt's children) operated as my brother and sister. Overall, I felt, and still feel, incredibly loved and I have a level of resilience that has served me well in my adult years. And while my aunt took care of me with equal love, care, and regard as if I was her child, it truly was something within me that always felt. . .extra.

Isn't that something? How two things can be true? How on the one hand, can you feel loved and cared for, but at the same time, can the circumstances of your situation and how you arrived there make you feel a certain way and you have to spend years of work unraveling through the complexities of it all?

I shared that I joined my aunt in her home around the age of 12. This also happens to be that magical age when you advance from middle school to high school. So, in addition to these general feelings I was having, I now had to contend with a major transition to a new school. It would be a major miss if I did not share how I actually claimed my spot to attend high school. I'll take you down the full journey of that in Chapter 3, but know that unlike the thousands of other kids from across the state of Michigan who "rightfully" claimed their spot by passing a mandatory standardized test to get in, I did not.

So my introduction to high school wasn't met with even a remote feeling of fitting in or with confidence or with the glow of possibility. It was actually more rooted in feeling like the extra kid, just trying to fit in both at home and at a new school. And while most ninth graders aren't oozing with leadership skills or even thinking of themselves as being a leader (a practice that I'm personally on a mission to change), whatever little bit of confidence freshmen have that leads them to want to join sports or an extracurricular group, or even feel like they could dream about what's next, I can't say that I felt like I had that.

I recently ran across my school ID card from my freshman year and noticed that my name was spelled incorrectly and remained that way for most of my high school experience. My lack of confidence manifested actions that resulted in me not thinking at that time that I was important enough or that the spelling of my name was something essential enough to be corrected.

Truth be told, I only went to my high school because that older sibling/cousin of mine, Derrick, had gone and graduated from there, and I only pursued an admissions test to college because one day a university was doing onsite admissions and my friends were doing it, so I thought, well, I guess I'll do that too. At that point, and for quite some time into my late teens and even into my 20s, I felt far from being a leader, far from having a vision for my life, and far from taking control of what I wanted to do next. And, while I know that I went back far in my life to my teen years to start to unravel where my earliest recollection of this incongruence with leadership was, that's what was necessary.

Since this book is dedicated to discovering, defining, and refining the leader within you, it may be necessary for you to take a visit of your own, in order for you to move forward, to recollect where you started not to feel like a leader or when something happened in your life that made you feel like being a leader just wasn't attainable. I made this mental journey for myself many years ago. When I truly reflect on how I felt then, I accept, acknowledge, and honor it, but I also align it with what I've accomplished, what I did and still do for others on their leadership journey, and I stay open to learning and advancing along the way.

Have you done that for yourself yet? Have you explored your personal historical journey and relationship with leadership?

Furthermore, while we're on our own personal history lessons about ourselves, let's just dive into our relationship with the word "leadership." According to the Macmillan Dictionary Blog, the word "leader" comes from the Old English word *laedan*, meaning "to go before as a guide." It was first used in English in the 14th century to describe a person in charge, and then various other uses came about later.

Take a moment and think about the multitude of things in our lives that were created or defined for one purpose, then evolved into being applicable for our ever-changing world. We really don't need to explore any further afield than how many of us are currently transported from one place to another, through shared transportation companies like DiDi, Grab, Lyft, Ola Cabs, or Uber.

There was a time when none of us could have fathomed climbing into a complete stranger's car to get to work, school, home, happy hour, or the airport. Fundamentally, without proper protocols, rules, and security in place, it's actually a terrible idea. But now it's an essential part of our everyday lives and mostly "safe" to do, and feels like second nature to do so.

While there was a time in history (and even still now) where we needed direction, complete guidance, and permission, humankind has evolved. There are more resources, opportunities, industries, and people than what existed in the 14th century, when that leadership definition was manifested.

So our relationship with the word "leader" is rooted in this age-old definition that leadership only works and applies if you are being guided, told what to do, and directed. Our relationship is rooted in the idea that you can't just raise your hand and proclaim that you are a leader.

But why not?

Why can't you say, "Yes, I'm a leader," and then utilize every day and every opportunity to refine those skills, understand our opportunities and commit to elevating? Why is it necessary to wait for permission to be a leader, especially when the very first opportunity to lead doesn't start with leading anyone else, but with you.

This declaration of leadership that you have the opportunity to make doesn't mean that you instantly get thrown into a pit of overwhelmingly leading other people from day one.

No one should be expected to be able to or even be remotely interested in leading a team of any number or group of individuals on day one of their leadership proclamation.

What if you're not quite ready to lead others, but you're still on a path to commit and declare yourself as a leader? Well, that's where leadership levels come into play.

Leadership opportunities conveniently come in levels, allowing you to declare yourself as one as you commit to continually refining your skills as you ascend to your next level.

Figure I.1 shows the four different levels that exist throughout our leadership elevation. While a visual of these four levels could be shown in a multitude of different ways, this image is depicted this way intentionally. Whether you decide to ascend beyond self-leadership to lead others, to lead communities, or even to lead movements, there will be one constant in these scenarios—and that is you. And, as you give yourself permission to lead in these areas, it'll be your continued responsibility to self-reflect, skill up, and prepare to be ready.

Also, I'd like for you to embrace the fact that the journey of leadership doesn't just exist within the walls of a corporate workplace. You don't see a diagram that is only valid if you're climbing a corporate ladder. Let me explain why.

Some of the greatest leaders are those we deeply admire who lead in social settings, who shine bright in our religious institutions, or who are even quietly spearheading a small committee at that

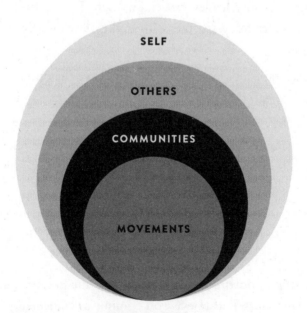

Figure I.1 Leadership levels.

volunteer human rights organization that most people have never heard of. And, quite frankly, there are more opportunities to lead socially and communitywide than what may be available at just your workplace. (I look forward to diving into that in Chapter 10, "Everyday Ways to Lead.")

Now, to be clear, leadership isn't this thing that you sign up for that you never revisit, work on, or work at. It can't be treated like another junk email list to send promotional material as you reap the benefits of the discounts. It won't serve you if it's handled like another package of salad spring mix that wastes away in your produce drawer. It has to be a commitment that you're working on, working at, and embracing every day.

In many ways, leadership and your personal journey in it is a lifelong commitment. And, if we're embracing the fact that change in our personal and professional lives is constant, then so are the opportunities to refine our inner leader.

Now that we've gotten comfortable with and see the value of embracing the unexpected and realize that there is a place for it in the world of your leadership journey, we've cleared the way to really get started.

The Unexpected Leader is your guide to discovering the leader within you, while also empowering you to take your next necessary step to elevate in your journey.

I want you to be firmly rooted in and solidly on the leadership acceptance or reacceptance journey. I say reacceptance because some of us have begun down a solid path and then something happens in our life that throws us off track, makes us question our abilities, or rocks our confidence to the core.

One or two bad annual reviews, a disagreement with a friend, a divorce, a child who doesn't want to hang with you anymore, or a planned girls' trip that didn't happen doesn't mean that you

now lose your leader badge or that you don't qualify to be a leader. Those experiences in life are exactly that—life experiences that we have the opportunity to navigate, learn from, and elevate out of. So whether you're just now giving yourself permission to be a leader or you're recommitting, there's space and opportunity for you.

This book is so important right and into the future because of the ever-evolving world around us. Our daily interactions and the world's innovations and advancement have the ability to improve the world around us and in many ways are doing so, but they also introduce new, unchartered territories, experiences, and challenges. We must be equipped with the right set of skills, tools, and empowerment to feel that we are capable of tackling these challenges.

Here are a few fundamental truths:

1. The world will continue to change.
2. The world is filled with people (like you) who can use their leadership skills to maximize and address these changes.
3. By being intentional about your growth and development opportunities, you can be the person who doesn't fold at the face of a change, but one who looks around to accept that there are opportunities all around you just waiting for you to take advantage of and take action on.

The first five chapters of this book are foundational. They provide you with the essential information to solidify yourself and arm you with the insight and inspiration to get on the leadership path. I will spend plenty of time in the second section on leadership elevation, which digs into the deep details and depth around leadership. The last section addresses some common pitfalls that you may experience along the way.

I must be clear and honest in saying that no two journeys are alike. (And that's okay.)

While my wish for you is that you will give yourself permission to both start and elevate in your leadership journey, know that there will be unknowns, there will be pitfalls, and there will be mistakes, but none of those things give you permission *not* to get started.

So, in your own unique way, whether it's saying it loud and proud, whispering it for just you to hear alone, declaring it on your social pages, or making a small note about it in this year's journal or planner, declare that you are a leader and that it's time to define and refine the leader within you.

Say this: *"Today, and every day I am a leader and I'm ready to take the journey to discover, define, and refine my leader within!"*

Okay, now let's really get started!

I What to Expect When You're Expecting Leadership

A commitment to debunking and demystifying leadership is what you can expect from this book.

And one of the best ways to do that is to let you know what to expect when you hop on board the leadership train (which, by the way, you're already on)!

Let's get started!

1 Making the Leadership Decision

Throughout our lives, we spend a significant amount of our time in a state of seeking approval and permission. Think about it—from asking permission to cross the street as a child to begging for a friend to stay the night, to school admissions processes, to securing a driver's license, to job interview opportunities to marriage licenses and passport approvals, we are constantly seeking approval to do things in our lives.

This chain of approvals that we seek starts early, usually with the teaching of the words and phrases "may I," "can I," and "please." Not only are we seeking approval, but we've been conditioned to then wait a certain amount of time for the approval of whatever it is that we asked for to be granted.

It should be no surprise that this waiting behavior carries over into other parts of our lives, even when it's not necessary. While there are times in our lives when patience needs to be activated, intentionally used, and practiced, there are moments—important moments—when we must take ownership, decide, and move forward. But so often we don't.

And one of the many reasons why we wait for this permission (outside of just being conditioned to do so) is because it's often hard to resonate with being or stepping into something that isn't a reflection of who we are, who we think we are, or who we believe we could be.

I mean, if no one has told you that you are a leader, that you have leadership potential, or that you have the opportunity to grow in your leadership journey, it's possible that you just never imagined the possibilities of being one.

Or perhaps you're not interested in even being associated with what mainstream leadership is often projected to be. Many of us have seen firsthand what it looks like for someone else to be hung out to dry publicly after a massive leadership snafu or mistake. We've seen the public "cancellation" of leaders of major organizations who've used insensitive words, put their personal financial interest above that of the company, or made unwanted passes and gestures to subordinates.

Some very public oustings include:

- Away co-founder Steph Korey, who left her position as CEO following a scathing report about the company's culture
- A major disagreement between the Expedia board and the C-suite, which sparked the abrupt departure of CEO Mark Okerstrom
- Steve Easterbrook being ousted as McDonald's CEO and president after the board determined that he violated company policy
- Nike CEO Mark Parker leaving his position, which was marred by two major scandals

But guess what else we've all seen and maybe even experienced? We've seen children falling off their bikes while figuring out how to transition out of training wheels. We've witnessed students failing out of college while trying to navigate their way through higher education. We've seen the successful marriage rate continually decline year over year over year. We've seen unfortunate and heartbreaking moments of witnessing fatal car crashes. We've heard of, seen, and experienced the most frustrating and inconveniencing travel delays by some of the world's largest airlines. We've seen people win millions of dollars, then ruin their lives by letting it reactivate their hidden vices and demons.

But we still try our hand at these things, when it is our turn. We're quick to say, "But I can do it better," or "I'll do things differently," or "Just let me give it a try."

Why aren't we willing to or hesitant to take this same "can do," "let me at 'em," "I can do it" approach to leadership? Why are we waiting for permission to elevate in our leadership journey or even just proudly declare ourselves as a self-leader?

Is it because you don't believe you're ready to lead, that you've never been affirmed in your leadership abilities, that you have no interest in leading other people, or you're concerned about making a mistake and being hung out to dry for the entire world to see?

I understand why anyone would want to hide out and avoid the spotlight if they knew that their entire life would be turned upside down by one mistake. But what if I told you that leadership is more than just a title?

What if you bought into the fact that leadership is a deeply personal journey, one that is rooted in ownership over your life, over your actions, and over the legacy and impact that you want to leave?

Some of the best leaders have actually never stepped foot into any executive office, never saw or craved the spotlight, and may periodically dress up, but they're not in possession of the latest tailored or custom suits, cars, or gaudy possessions and have no interest in them.

What if I told you—and you believed—that your commitment to seeing yourself as a leader opens unknown doors for you, allows you to connect with your peers and colleagues better, and helps you to authentically pave the way for yourself and for other leaders following in your footsteps?

I'll be the first to reveal that our leadership journey is both a complex and simple word and concept.

It is complex because it has many components that have a role within it, yet it's also simple. This is a good thing because multiple components means that there are multiple opportunities to work on elements that then help you to be a better leader. If there were only one or two things and you just couldn't seem to master or make any progress on them and those were the only options that you had, you may be quickly frustrated and decide that this leadership thing just isn't for you or you don't have what it takes to be a leader. But that's not the case. There are a multitude of different areas to dig into in the leadership realm.

On the other hand, leadership is simple because the decision to embark on this journey starts with you and you alone. It's your decision, your choice, and reliant on you to chart the path.

The components and characteristics of leadership are behaviors and skills that we experience and master every day. But without the necessary focus, intent, and finesse, the things that we've mastered can easily not equal the outcome of being a good leader. But why is that?

Consider one of your favorite recipes. Think about its core ingredients and the essential parts of it that make it your favorite. Mine is lobster macaroni, the cheesiest of the cheesiest macaroni with a wealth of all the cheeses, finished with an ever so lightly brown crusted top.

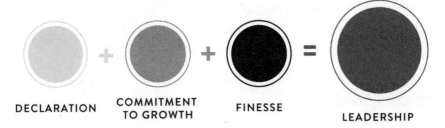

DECLARATION   COMMITMENT TO GROWTH   FINESSE   LEADERSHIP

Figure 1.1 The leadership equation.

It's not enough for me to perfectly measure out and set aside the necessary ingredients and assume that just because I combine these ingredients in a bowl and even place it into the oven at just the right temperature, that the outcome I am seeking will be achieved. It takes some finesse, in the form of whisking the egg, sifting some flour, poaching the lobster, blanching the broccoli. It's the finesse of it all that results in the delicious outcome.

If you are anything like me, at this point in the conversation we start looking for some sort of guide, graphic, or rendering to see how this leadership finesse concept comes to life. Figure 1.1 shows just that.

If the leadership equation is a combination of declaring that you are a leader, committing to the journey, and adding a sprinkle of finesse, you may be wondering, "Why don't we just break apart this seemingly simple equation and lay out the components?"

Well, I'm glad you inquired, because that's what we're going to do throughout this book, and we'll get started on that right now by defining what each component of the leadership equation means.

The Declaration

Making a declaration and accepting the fact that you are qualified to be a leader is likely a lot simpler than you may think it to be. When the weight and hesitation of making (or remaking) this declaration starts to rear its head, there are a couple of things that you have at your disposal: accepting change and embracing an accountability crew.

Accepting Change

The only thing that is constant in our lives is change. While we often work immensely hard to have a certain level of consistency and stability, it is always just a façade and temporary. Change will always return to us and, unfortunately, often at the most inopportune times. When this change happens, it will be up to us to reach inside of our leadership toolkit to pull out the skills and the reminders we need to elevate or just keep going.

As both a self-leader and a leader of others, the acceptance of change is a key component of our journey. This acceptance allows us to avoid shying away from change, but anticipate and accept that it will occur at some point in our lives and likely much sooner than expected. Also, we must accept that change can be two-sided. There is change that is crushing and challenging, but there is also change that is welcoming, pleasant, and often needed in our lives. From the moment we are born, we are consistently evolving through a world of seen and unseen changes. Accepting that change will occur enables us to be more prepared for it when it does occur.

In order to really address change, I have to go deep with you for a moment. Follow me.

Not only must we recognize that change is happening all around us all the time and that it may be initiated by outside factors that we have no control over, but there is another approach to change that we have the opportunity to be the initiator of: change that we lead and champion within and for the benefit of us.

Although change is far from a new concept and keeps happening to us over and over and over again in our personal and professional lives, we have all struggled with it.

It was (and still is) such a challenge for us that in 1977 psychologists James O. Prochaska and Carlo Di Clemente created the Transtheoretical Model (TTM) of Behavior Change, also called the Stages of Change Mode, which assesses an individual's readiness to act on a new healthier behavior, and provides strategies or processes of change to guide the individual.

As part of this model, there are six stages that guide someone to actually experience sustainable change:

1. **Precontemplation:** People do not intend to take action in the foreseeable future (defined as within the next six months). People are often unaware that their behavior is problematic or produces negative consequences. People in this stage often underestimate the pros of changing behavior and place too much emphasis on the cons.

2. **Contemplation:** People are intending to start healthy behavior in the foreseeable future (defined as within the next six months). People recognize that their behavior may be problematic, and a more thoughtful and practical consideration of the pros and cons of changing the behavior takes place, with equal emphasis placed on both. Even with this recognition, people may still feel ambivalent toward changing their behavior.

3. **Preparation** (Determination): People are ready to take action within the next 30 days. People start to take small steps toward the behavior change, and they believe changing their behavior can lead to a healthier life.

4. **Action:** People have recently changed their behavior (defined as within the last six months) and intend to keep moving forward

with that behavior change. People may exhibit this by modifying their problem behavior or acquiring new healthy behaviors.

5. **Maintenance:** People have sustained their behavior change for a while (defined as more than six months) and intend to maintain the behavior change going forward. People in this stage work to prevent relapse to earlier stages.

6. **Termination:** People have no desire to return to their unhealthy behaviors and are sure they will not relapse. Since this is rarely reached and people tend to stay in the maintenance stage, this stage is often not considered applicable in many situations.

While change can certainly be more abrupt and occur quickly, most changes in behavior, especially habitual behavior, occur continuously through a cyclical repeating process.

While there are always limitations to any model, even the TTM, this model is worth knowing as we explore the world of leadership because many of the behaviors that we may or may not possess as we commit to growth on our journey may be ones that we've attempted to unsuccessfully tackle in the past.

Change often takes time.

My ask is that as you commit to growth that you will be patient and realistic with the work that you'll need to do to unwind behaviors and practices that may have been in play for 5, 10, 15, 20, 30, or more years.

Accountability Crew

While self-motivation and self-accountability are a joy to have, there's nothing wrong with enlisting the support of an accountability crew. These are the people who remind you of your goals, elevate your thinking, and help you to see your possibilities, especially your opportunities within your leadership realm.

While Chapter 12, "Building Your Tribe," goes deeper into how you do this, I'd like to offer some initial insight to ensure that you're beginning to think about the two ways this accountability crew could show up in your life.

1. **Unintentionally, before you fully commit to the leadership journey:** There are people all around us each and every day who are silently rooting for us, championing us, and opening doors. As much as it doesn't always seem that way and you may feel alone on whatever journey you are on, these people and this support is around you. Your role is to reflect on it and tap into it. Think about some of these people who exist in your world and who are around you:
   (a) Anyone you consider a mentor
   (b) Friends who ask about how your job is going and what's next for you
   (c) A past teacher or boss who went that extra mile to help you see what's possible or what you're capable of
   (d) A random unknown person who just sees the possibilities in you that maybe you can't even see.
      I want you to think about who these people are around you. Accept that you have the support that you need to elevate further in your leadership journey. Now it's your turn to take the baton and move forward.

2. **Intentionally and knowingly,** which will be what you'll curate to help you continue to elevate in your journey, avoid pitfalls, and transparently challenge you when necessary. While it's nice to have a support system around that organically and sometimes accidentally fell into place, your continued growth will rely on you being intentional about the continued cultivation of this support. Your impact opportunities and growth shouldn't be just left to chance. It's time for you to actively go after it by enlisting a crew of support around you.

Commitment to Growth

I must take this moment to remind you that while you're on your leadership journey (which you are because you're reading this book!), it is not necessary for you to know it all. As a matter of fact, it's impossible (and unnecessary) for you to know it all, so trying to do so is a complete waste of time.

What you can do and what is fruitful is committing to growing every single day. The skills you need on day one of your leadership journey will be far different from the skills you need and that are required on day one thousand. Also, as you elevate to different opportunities, that commitment to continued growth that you make early in your journey will be most handy. One of the larger mistakes people make is that they start to get elevation opportunities, but then shy away from their growth commitment. This is a fatal mistake. We must be willing to continuously learn and grow as we elevate to new opportunities and spaces.

Just because you have arrived in a new space based on your previous accomplishments does not mean that you are now immune from learning the new skill and tools that will help you be your best at this new level and help you continue to rise and elevate.

I'll explore a myriad of different ways you can commit to and identify growth opportunities with the "Leadership Elevation" portion of this book. For now, just know that this commitment is necessary.

Finesse

Leadership in all its glory can often be villainized and come with a dark cloud above it. It can be nuanced and heavy, because there is a disconnect between the historical *definitions* and depictions of leadership and the accessibility and relatability of it to the everyday human.

In other words, it's like every other thing in the world. If you can't see, understand, or believe in the possibility of it, it's mighty hard for you to align with being it. Furthermore, humans are good and complicated. Therefore, the element of finesse is necessary.

Finesse can be regarded in a couple of different ways. I want you to first think of it as a tweak, a customization, or a unique approach. Your finesse allows you to meet ever-changing personal, professional, and unknown qualities of others as we navigate both our self-leadership journey and the level that we will impact for others.

In Chapter 8 I dive deeply into the world of finessing your leadership style. It is there that I'll explore how to fine-tune and modify your style and leadership approach, so it can meet the needs of all the complicated humans looking to you for guidance as well as understanding how and when you should modify your needs to meet the goals that you are going after.

Now that we know that we have more of a say in our leadership journey and decision than we often give ourselves credit for, let's close out this very first chapter by owning that decision. Before we advance to the honest nuances of leadership, let's decide together to choose leadership.

Yes, there are some things in life for which we must wait for permission, but choosing to fully step into our leadership journey is not one of those things. Also, since I know that leadership can feel like a heavy and deep subject, I want to assure you that you aren't alone. That's what this book is for—to guide and support your ever-growing and ever-changing leadership journey and needs.

So, while we did agree in the book's introduction that today and every day you are a leader (you agreed to that, right?), I'd like for you to remember that you have the power time and time again to make a leadership declaration and commit to continued growth and finesse as needed.

Since change will occur at some point in our lives, it will be necessary to remind yourself that you can jump back fully in your leadership journey and growth at any point in time.

Okay, now let's jump into those known, unknown, and nuanced elements of leadership.

2 The Nuances of Leadership

Humans are far from simple.

Our stark and distinct differences in background, preferences, experiences, and desires make us naturally multifaceted. Here are some other humanoid facts that make the 7.5 billion people in the world unique and nuanced:

- Over 4,300 different religions exist.
- There are over 650 ethnic groups across 190 countries.
- There are roughly 6,500 languages spoken in the world.
- There are 16 different personality types that someone can embody.
- There are 5 racial categories.

The way that humans exist organically means that the way that we develop, connect, grow, and elevate must also have a bit of complexity to it, *even a healthy dose of nuance.*

But nuances complicate things. Wouldn't it be easier if leadership was as simple as 1 + 1? Wouldn't it be easier if the steps, processes, and formulas to lead were always laid out perfectly and worked in every single situation, every single time?

Well, is simplicity really what we aspire to and desire?

Many of us end up with a level of simplicity in our lives and then we crave the one thing that we don't think we want, but we do. We could call this a craving for variation, differences, uniqueness, and/or change. To keep us all on the same page, let's call it nuance, which essentially means a subtle difference in something.

I want you to take a small mental trip into your closet where your shoes live. You may be visualizing several pairs of shoes, many of which are the same color and similar in style. If you're a true shoe lover, you may even start to let your mind wander to other shoes that you recently saw online that you want to add to the collection. If you're being completely honest, do you really *need* this new pair, or do you just like the flashy buckles, attractive soles, or exposed zipper that your other ones don't have?

It's no surprise that one of the things that we need for leadership to be effective is woven into the fabric of who we are, what we crave and what we need: nuance. Let's explore more of the nuances of leadership and how to utilize and manage them throughout our journey.

Leaders Don't Always Need to Be Out Front

It feels good to be recognized, highly regarded, and regaled. Who doesn't want to be celebrated! *I know I do.*

Even people who don't necessarily crave the spotlight like to be highlighted in some capacity for the right thing and when the time is right. But always being highly regarded and celebrated isn't the most important aspect of leadership, or even a goal at all.

When you take on the responsibility and commitment to embrace and elevate in your leadership journey, you also accept that everything isn't always about you or about you being personally celebrated. It's often about the bigger picture, the greater goal, and not just your own growth and development but that of others as well.

Leadership Tip: For those of you who were fearful that this was the case, take a breather. See, there is space for you to lead and develop into a greater leader without always being the center of attention. In just a short while, we will venture into the world of different leadership styles. Keep your eyes on both the democratic and coaching leadership styles because they will likely resonate with you quite a bit.

If I'm being honest here, this is an area of leadership that I've had to refine for myself over time and here's how I do it. I am a fan of the details, not necessarily organically by choice, but instead because of my first entrepreneurial foray. I co-founded a wedding and event production company in the early 2000s, and while that experience left me with a wealth of memories, experiences, and skills, it also left me with a unique skill set that is both beneficial and *stifling*.

Leadership Tip: It is our responsibility to identify and be honest when certain skills that once served you no longer serve you or are only beneficial every now and then.

It is the ability to be deeply immersive into details—details that many people would not think to pay attention to or amplify. This deep immersion in details usually positions me to be out front, to be the "face" of situations, to be the point person, and to be the one who usually has the answers or knows where to get them.

Because I started my professional career in this way and became known for this skill and happen to be really good at it, it has continued to permeate into other parts of my career as well, usually positioning me as the leader, the point person, and the one who will likely have the answer.

While this skill has served me well over the years, it carries an inherent deep-seated challenge. It positions me always to be out front, in times and in situations when I could or should play the back seat. It also does the exact opposite of what I personally strive to do through my leadership consultancy, Scarlet—empower other people to embrace their leadership abilities and advance to their next level.

Because, if I am busy, always in front, always taking the lead, always being the default person with all the answers, I'm not leaving the space and opportunity for other people to refine their skills, serve as the one "out front" person, and have their fair share of leadership mistakes and growth that will enable them to elevate themselves in their journey. The other question is "How can a leader (like you) grow and thrive and elevate to their next level if they aren't making space, time, and opportunity for the collection of new skills and leadership abilities that they need for what's ahead of them?" Remember that leadership doesn't need to be boastful, shiny, bright, and out front all the time. Leave the space for both you and the others around you to grow by taking a supportive side seat or back seat sometimes.

Take the Back Seat

Instead of being the first person to answer questions, ask if anyone else has input, feedback, or perspective before offering yours. It empowers people to speak freely without the pressure of feeling like what they say will conflict with what you just said.

Leaders Don't Always Need Followers

While most leaders are characterized as having a mass of people they direct, lead, or guide, there is an essential step that must happen for you to effectively lead other people, other things, or organizations. It's the ability and commitment to lead yourself, every day and in every way.

Figure 2.1 shows the leadership levels you need to be aware of and also lets you see that there is more to your leadership journey beyond just leading masses of people.

Embracing the fact that one of the most important leadership levels is the leadership of self is an important foundational learning. Before you can advance to be a dynamic people leader or the leader of an organization, movement, or community, embracing your role as a self-leader is a pivotal step. My greatest hope for you is that you

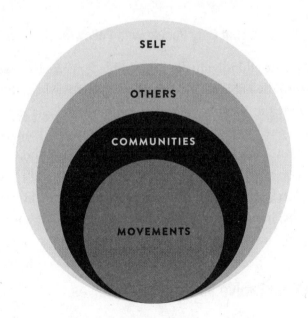

Figure 2.1 Levels of leadership.

appreciate and embrace the most important leadership level as the leader of self. At this level, you don't need followers and that's quite alright. Leading yourself still qualifies you to be a leader.

While we're here, though, I do want to expand on this leadership level concept since it is hugely the basis for so many concepts throughout the book. Let me give you a breakdown of what types of entities fit within each category.

Self	Others	Communities	Movements
This is all you.	Direct reports Children Grandchildren Peers at work Friends	PTA Homeowners' association Entrepreneurship groups Fitness groups	Religious institutions Equal rights organizations

Overcome the Idea That Only People with Followers Are Leaders

Although we are all individually responsible for ourselves, we can easily fall into the habit of not directing our paths where they need to go. We fall prey to autopilot actions within our life as a result of doing that—not leading ourselves. And, to lead you, you actually do not need any followers, you just need you. As you get better at self-leadership and begin to acquire and refine your skills within that leadership level, you may start to feel more confident about leading others and begin down that path. But all alone you are a leader who is responsible for leading yourself.

Leaders Must Evolve as the World Evolves

Heading into 2020, many leaders across the globe had an arsenal of tools and skills at their fingertips that were relevant, meaningful, and impactful. Once March of 2020 rolled around, many leaders quickly realized that the skills that they needed to manage themselves and the people they were leading wasn't sufficient. I intentionally discussed change in Chapter 1 at great length. And that won't be the last time you hear that word in this book. As a matter of fact, I'm about to talk about it again right now.

The evolution of the world is rapidly shifting every day. Environmental, social, and demographic changes directly impact us as everyday leaders. We can't be oblivious to the world changing while also committing to being good leaders because it's all connected. The tricky part of these changes is that what might be a really big factor of the world in 10, 7, or even 2 years could be completely unknown to anyone on earth. While pandemics were not unheard of, most of the world wasn't waiting in the wings for the next one to occur. *Well, I'm sure that the world's top epidemiologists are always waiting and planning for this.* But most of us were completely caught off guard and weren't ready.

Leaders must pay attention, adjust, and embrace the realities of the world so that our skills and abilities, and the application of them, can be adjusted accordingly.

Consider the leaders who have historically only been focused on results from their teams and that approach may have worked for them for years. Well, around mid-March of 2020, they needed to become more tuned in to mental health, to emotional awareness, and to more than just team results in order for their department and their organization to be effective.

Effective leaders can't put their heads in the sand and avoid the ever-changing world around them and the skills needed to address the challenges of modern times.

Avoid the Error of Not Evolving

There are a multitude of companies and leaders who have failed to remain relevant and effective because of their inability to evolve with the world's changes. But, since I'd rather not scare you off with a fear tactic so early in this book, let me take a different approach.

Think about how you once handled conflict in your life.

Were you once someone who took an aggressive approach despite the people involved, the situation dynamics. or the desired direction outcome?

Or was there a period in your life where you didn't seek or acknowledge feedback from others and it cost you time, money, energy, or unnecessary stress?

When you get an inkling that you are stagnant, stuck, or not reaching your full leadership potential, don't ignore it—take action.

Realize You Won't Make Everyone Happy

While it brings me no joy, splendor, or happiness to discuss this area, it's my job. I can't be an effective or good leadership evangelical in this space if I'm not willing to share the warm, fuzzy, nuanced, and controversial areas of leadership, so here goes.

Being a leader is not synonymous with making everyone happy.

Are there immense benefits? Absolutely! But leadership is not always bright, shiny, happy, and glorious. But what it can and should be is deeply aligned with your greater goals and intended leadership legacy (which we will explore in Chapter 4). Your goals and maybe even your organization's goals may not be the same as other people's that you encounter. So that in itself may cause tension.

You can't always ignore this tension. It may require you to address these things head on and may not make everyone happy, but that's a reality of leadership. Also, when you can nudge another growing leader out of their comfort zone, there may be some discomfort as well. But remember, if we're personally stuck at a certain level, we can't elevate. What may be needed is the cultivation of another leader around you so that you have the space and bandwidth to grow and elevate and so do they.

While there will likely be some long-term happiness, appreciation, and fulfillment on the part of the person that you uprooted out of their stagnant comfort zone, this initial nudging that you do may not be received so well. We'll dive into leadership blueprints, style, and approaches later, but let's just accept that your declaration and commitment to leading won't always make everyone happy. But keep your long-term goals and legacy in mind while navigating leadership, because that is the more important focus.

Before we jump into discovering the leader within you in Chapter 3, I want to ensure that you are aware of the realities and nuances of leadership that can sometimes catch us off guard and often derail us completely.

These nuances aren't prevalent enough to outweigh the goals that you have for your life and career. When I go through the leadership legacy exercise later on in Chapter 4, you'll quickly see that. This world that we're in is filled with nuance, changes, adjustments, and unknowns. Give yourself permission to go after what you want on your leadership journey, but with eyes wide open that nuances will be right there with you.

Also, consider this. Whether or not you're embracing your leadership potential and opportunities, you still won't make everyone around you happy. So, since this conflict will exist either way, wouldn't it be more prudent to be intentional and to take ownership over your leadership journey, versus just letting things happen to happen to you?

The final insight I'd like to offer in this chapter is about the conundrum and nuance between manager and leader. There is often nothing more nuanced than the interchangeability of our word choices and selections. Let's take a moment to address a misnomer around a few often interchangeable words.

The words "boss" and "manager" have likely been part of our vocabulary for eons. But let's dive into them a bit. Boss and manager could be considered leaders by default, but most of us have had experiences where that is not the case. A person who is a boss or a manager is not always a leader. Before we jump full into the different types of leadership styles, let's first make sure you're clear on the differences between managing and leading.

Although it is more effective, most efficient, and the most optimal situation when there is alignment between someone being a leader and a manager or boss, this is not always the case. Depending on the type of organization, there is preferred verbiage that describes how a superior is titled. While there are other terms, the most common ones are:

- Manager
- Supervisor

This is the perfect time to lay out the difference between a manager/supervisor and a leader.

Managers do exactly what the root word implies: they manage. At the core, managers are focused on getting things done day to day. They manage schedules, processes and procedures, projects, and performance. They are usually focused on short-term goals, resolving work issues, and enforcing company or situational policies.

A leader leads. A leader creates an environment, a culture, and situations where people want to follow them. They influence and they inspire people to take action. They create a culture driven by solid values and they consistently model behavior that's in the best interest of the individual and the organization.

The Manager as Leader

In the best possible scenario, a superior is someone who takes into account the importance of getting the work done (whatever the work is) and also understands the great responsibility and opportunity to lead at the same time.

Not All Leaders Are Managers

Self-leadership is at the core of leading. It's the simple concept that leadership starts with you, not when you are designated with subordinates. Regardless of whether you have the opportunity or great responsibility of having subordinates on your team, you have the opportunity to be a leader—a self-leader.

The Downfall of Managing Without Leading

There are mostly missed opportunities when someone manages without leading. Humans are complicated beings who are motivated, inspired, and driven in different ways. Taking the management-only approach takes none of that into account. A leader who is committed to leading and not just managing recognizes that there is an opportunity to get to the end goal while also inspiring and providing development opportunities to a direct report at the same time.

Now, onward to finding that leader that already exists within you.

3 Discovering the Leader Within You

Sad news ahead . . .

My father passed away in September of 2021 and although, yes, tears and grief were on the menu, an unexpected discovery happened in the fray of planning for a funeral and wrapping up funeral commitments. While going through some of his belongings, a brown paper bag with a slight stench of mildew was uncovered. When I was told that something was found that I might be interested in seeing, I couldn't even imagine what this mystery package might be. My dad had a reputation of being—how do I say this—a collector of things that weren't his.

To be more specific, he always managed to get his hands on and stash away family pictures, keepsakes, and things that were one of a kind and not his. To my surprise, this mystery item that he had stashed away was a rather alarming stack of certificates. This wasn't just any stack of certificates, but ones that spanned back to preschool from my beloved K–8 elementary school, Myra Jones, historically

situated on the east side of Detroit. It was also an interesting
discovery because as a child, we had a house fire and these certificates
were thought to have been ruined by fire, smoke, and water damage
(hence the mildew smell).

Now, before I go further into why this bag of certificates was so
alarming, let me peel back a few more layers of my story. After I left
Myra Jones, I graduated from Cass Technical High School, one of the
most celebrated and well-known high schools in the state of Michigan
(and beyond). Most attendees are regarded for their academic
abilities, especially since entry into the school requires each student to
successfully pass a standardized test. If there is anything that I can
point to as my "kryptonite," it would be *any* standardized test.

In my lifetime, I distinctly recall these anxiety-inducing tests—
the CAT (California Achievement Test), the MEAP (Michigan
Educational Assessment Program, ACT (American College Testing),
and SAT (Scholastic Aptitude Test). I'll also transparently say that
I distinctly recall never doing very well on any of these tests. This also
included the Examination High School Test, which was required for
admission to Cass. This test was designed as a pass or fail situation
and I absolutely failed.

Now, I did say that I actually *graduated* from Cass but also that
I didn't pass the test to get in. Well, the truth is that my entry into
Cass wasn't based on my academic abilities, but instead my
performance abilities. The high school had a mostly unknown process
of allowing students who had performance abilities to audition their
way in, so since I had vocal abilities, I auditioned my way in.

Once I was inside the school walls, there wasn't some magical
breakthrough where I academically began to pummel my way
through the crowd and ascend to new scholarly heights. I was on
academic probation one semester because I received a 1.9 GPA.
(Whew, that's hard to even think about, let alone share and relive.)

Although I did make my way through Cass and proceeded to college, I did so in a manner that felt very jagged, unstructured, and quite frankly unsmart. If you ever asked me to describe myself with any kind of academic considerations in mind, I'd admit that I just wasn't that smart in high school. I went out of my way to let this be known in many conversations earlier in my life.

So, to return to those certificates in my father's possession, I was incredibly surprised. Now, I'm aware these weren't any earth-shattering set of awards, but that's the thing. Even for "simple" accolades, I was surprised to have been awarded them.

Now, why is that?

At what point in my life did I start to think that I wasn't astute or deserving enough to have received recognition in my youth? Well, I think this mental state developed over time, but I must say that my time in high school (some of the most important developmental times in a young person's life) molded mine.

While I had clearly spent this time collecting these seemingly well-deserved awards for seven or eight years, something happened in the following four years that completely dismantled this reality. That something for me was high school. Cass was a competitive, eclectic school that rewarded academic excellence (as most schools do). For me—someone who hadn't traditionally "earned" their spot in that school and who was now a super small fish in a massive pond of over a thousand "smart" freshmen from across the city of Detroit, any flicker of intelligence that might have been burning inside me was dimmed for many years.

This "unsmart" feeling carried on with me through college, into starting my first business, and even beginning a highly impactful executive career at one of the nation's largest nonprofits (more on that later) and a host of other things. Although what I had considered accomplishments were achieved, this feeling of low intelligence that

I had embraced seamlessly bled over into and impacted a critical area of my life—leadership.

For me, although I am what you call a self-starter (not afraid to start things or experiment with new opportunities), any success that came along with that experimentation had been historically categorized (in my mind) as luck, happenstance, or some magical occurrence that had nothing to do with my intelligence or aptitude.

This is probably why I deeply enjoy the podcast *How I Built This*. At the end of every episode, host Guy Raz asks his featured guest, "How much of your journey is attributed to luck versus hard work"? Of course, the guest responses vary deeply depending on who they are and their own personal perceptions, but that question always resonates with me deeply because I've had to revisit that question over and over again while wading through my own leadership journey.

It wasn't until I started writing my first leadership book that I began to realize the need to question these feelings and perceptions of myself. I mean, how could I effectively write a leadership book with the goal of empowering and tooling other people to elevate in their journey if I still had this sketchy view of my own leadership abilities? How is it possible that I didn't quite feel like a leader even though I had this track record of starting a couple of companies, ascending through some corporate leadership ranks, collecting some awards, and being consistently asked to be a mentor and advisor to many?

Giving Yourself Permission

I hadn't given myself permission to discover, define, and refine the leader within me. For all of those years, I was operating on autopilot, just doing and going and not really saying (to myself or to others), "I'm a leader, so let me do as such and act as such." I had subconsciously been embracing this narrative that where I'm at today is a product of luck and happenstance, not a reflection of my intelligence or leadership abilities.

And, luckily now, many places across the world are more embracing of the reality that your abilities and potential in life doesn't mean that you have to be the most academically astute or the most outgoing or the loudest voice in the room. Your potential in life is more than just a collection of how you did on a series of school tests filled with information that you may or may not ever see again.

Furthermore, this quote from former First Lady Michelle Obama wraps it up even more eloquently: *"If my future were determined just by my performance on a standardized test, I wouldn't be here. I guarantee you that."*

And, even if you were a standardized test warrior and found yourself in the top percentile of those assessments, that doesn't always clear you from the litany of "unsmart" feelings that we latch onto as we navigate our academic journeys, our corporate escapades, and our social circles. We begin to just get in the race (whatever the race is at the moment, from family to career) and not take ownership of our leadership journey, abilities, and potential.

Now that I've bared my soul and secrets, it's your turn. Let's talk about the leader within you. Consider this: Where have you been minimizing your leader within? Do you attribute your accolades and wins to pure luck instead of considering that some of your outcomes must be attached to some level of your work, intellect, and input?

Leadership is a vast topic that encapsulates many skills. I'll explore these topics throughout the book, but they all fall within these six core areas:

1. Self-awareness
2. Personality traits

3. Communication

4. Agility and adaptability

5. Delegation

6. Innovation and change maker

Within each of these six areas, there are a myriad of subtopics to explore, but there is also a very essential fact that must be embraced and understood. If you know that you've spent years and maybe even decades not embracing your role as a leader and attributing your positive outcomes to everything under the sun except for yourself, you may need to revisit this chapter a few times (and that's okay).

We don't spend years doing something and then, like magic, the effects of that thing just suddenly go away. Let's accept that just like we've committed to being on this leadership journey going forward, our past actions can also be a journey from which we must give ourselves permission to emerge.

When you find yourself not feeling like a leader, not believing that you are a leader, not operating in a way that gets you from where you are to where you want to be based on your leadership assessment, revisit this chapter and remind yourself that there is a leader within you and you deserve to and have the power to rediscover, refine, and redefine the leader within you.

Let's now explore a topic that is very rarely discussed but is often the missing piece needed to ground you, to keep you focused, and to intentionally direct your next leadership step and opportunities—your leadership legacy.

While we don't talk a lot today about our overall legacy, let alone our leadership legacy, understanding what it is for yourself allows you to make better decisions and allows you to further commit to your overall journey.

4 Creating Your Leadership Legacy

The word "legacy" can be heavy. With just one six-letter word, you could be forced to reflect on your entire life: what it has been thus far, what you're currently doing, and what you want the rest to be. And, depending on where you are in life right now, evaluating and reflecting on that can be unnerving. Our lives are filled with twists, turns, adjustments, unexpected situations, and surprises. So any perfectly laid plan has the potential of not going to plan at all.

When you think about legacy, you may be discouraged and decide not to think about it at all. But I encourage you to think about it fully, to embrace it, and even to welcome unexpected situations, which we explored in detail in previous chapters.

Your legacy is bigger than the past, the present, or the rest of your life. It's actually inclusive of the impact that you have the ability to make well beyond when your physical time here on earth is complete. You have a unique opportunity to dream, to plan, and to bring to life what you want your legacy to be—your leadership legacy.

Before we dive into this chapter, I want you to give yourself permission to take off the weight and overwhelming feeling that the word "legacy" can invoke. When reading this word or hearing it spoken, resist the urge to get worked up with negative self-talk. Don't succumb to what legacy may mean to someone else or even to society at large. I want this to be fully about you because, well, it is.

A legacy is not something that some people get to leave behind and others don't. A legacy is not exclusive to people who have reached a certain threshold, career level, or financial stature. Do you know how I know this is true? Think about someone in your life who has been highly disappointing, someone you may have looked up to or trusted with your valued secrets, but they betrayed your trust. Consider that someone for whom you had high hopes but they repeatedly let you down. This person has left an impact on your life. They probably left a negative impression and that is unfortunately what their legacy is to you.

I challenge you also to think about someone who has been monumental in your life. They've shown up for you. They've been a valued role model. They've been a valued resource to you time and time again. This person has also left an impression and your ongoing thoughts of them will likely be filled with happy memories. That is the legacy that they've left in your eyes.

For me, I immediately go back to my third-grade teacher, Ms. Leanna Jackson. Every chance I get, I thank this woman. She is singlehandedly the reason why I am confident enough to grace a stage, use my voice, and make an impact across the globe. She coached, trained, and mentored me into being someone who is not afraid of public speaking, who doesn't shy away from any microphone, and who understands the monumental power of using your voice, intentionally. Because of her, I can confidently do the work that I choose to do and feel good talking about it publicly. You've likely never heard of Ms. Leanna Jackson and you'll probably never meet her. But the legacy and impact this woman left on me and many of my classmates can't be matched. She's never won a Nobel Prize, was never recognized by any educational awards program, and has chosen to retire quietly and privately, but she too has a legacy—a monumental one. There are probably people in your life who have a parallel impact that Ms. Jackson had on me. And, while you could go through life hoping you might impact someone's life in that way, wishing you could leave that kind of mark or simply just wanting your life to be a good, solid reflection of positively impacting others, I can give you a different and significantly more effective approach.

What if you didn't leave any of this to chance at all? What if, instead of hoping, wishing, and dreaming, you intentionally charted a path to create a legacy that encompassed what you want your life to be a reflection of?

What if you committed to carefully crafting your own leadership legacy?

Legacies aren't magically manifested. They're created day by day and decision by decision, intentionally. They're formed, molded, shaped, and brought to life. And, since you've already committed to being a leader and charting a path to elevate your journey, you're already qualified to create this legacy.

Your Life Thesis

Now is the perfect time to double down on where you can show up as a leader. I talked about the legacy you have the opportunity to leave on others, but I need to bring us back to our leadership levels. We not only have the opportunity to impact others, communities, and movements, but we also have the most important opportunity to be impactful to ourselves, intentionally.

Creating Impact for You

The single most important person in your life is you. Now, I know that many of you who are reading this are parents, grandparents, aunts, uncles, siblings, cousins, and dear loved ones to many people in your life. And in many ways you may regard someone else's life more than that of your own. I'm not here to necessarily discourage you from your thinking, but instead encourage you to realize that if you aren't taken care of, empowered, lifted up, and in alignment with your own personal approach to balance, it's really hard to show up in the lives of others. When you do show up as a self-leader, guess who sees that, has the opportunity to model that, and begin their own leadership journey—the other people you regard so highly in your life.

So your leadership legacy can be fittingly based on the impact you want to have on other people, but it also very much lends itself to the impact that you want reflected in your own life based solely on you and the life you want to live.

I hope you're now thinking, "Well, what's next? How is this leadership legacy actually created? Let me pop the hood on one of the most important parts of my own journey to help set the stage for your next step.

Although I've personally had an opportunity to sit in and impact many spaces from wedding and event production to modern etiquette to leadership to corporate innovation, I decided many years ago that the only way that I could remain grounded, focused, and sane is by operating from a life thesis. My Life Thesis is a simple yet effective way to stay in tune with what's important to me, what my core values are, and why I make the decisions I make. For a person whose mind is always moving a million miles per hour, it's essential that I have a North Star and guiding post to help me stay on track. I invite you to embrace this practice, as it has served me incredibly well over the past 10 years. To ensure that you can create a leadership legacy that you can be proud of and stay committed to, let's first start with developing your Life Thesis (Figure 4.1). I created this guide for people who are curious about being intentional about what they are doing with their life, how they are doing it, and if it is truly fulfilling.

Life Thesis

Composing your Life Thesis is both an opportunity and an essential exercise.
We have 168 hours in a week. When you think of that, you may or *should* immediately wonder,
"Where does all of my time go."

Right along side that 168 hours is another daunting number, which is 35,000. That's the
average number of decisions each of us makes every day. *(That's a lot, right?)*

So, when you are faced with making so many decisions every day, the question is...
"What guides your decisions? What set of principles, North Star, or check points do you utilize
to help you keep going and elevate?"

Introducing... your *Life Thesis.*

CONSTRUCTING YOUR LIFE THESIS

Below are a list of questions, prompts, and a template to construct your Life Thesis.
As you give yourself permission to start and experience new things, this simple yet
impactful statement will guide you and support your next decision.

What keeps positively showing up in your life?	What are you really good at?

With no judgment, no fears, and no limits, who do you want to be?	What deeply moves and motivates you?

Your Life Thesis
When it's all said and done, my life will be a reflection of

_____

*I encourage you to take time over the next couple of weeks to answer these questions and plug them into your
Life Thesis template. Your thesis will evolve, change, and elevate over time, but commit to having a draft in place
within 14 days of starting, then editing as needed.*

Figure 4.1 Life Thesis.

While the Life Thesis itself can be a guiding force in your life, the elements of it are fairly simple. I recognize that a tool I'm proposing you use to guide your entire life can seem heavy and feel like it needs to be an entire novel, but consider this. A lot of the components of the Life Thesis are already answered for. They're in your head and need to be documented and organized in order to best serve you.

The Life Thesis has four essential components:

1. **Reflection of recurring events.** The question *What keeps positively showing up in your life?* helps you to make an accurate and informed list of your personal recurring events and themes in your life.

2. **Assessment of your strong skills.** The simple yet effective question *What are you good at?* allows you to do a personal data dump of the things that you thrive and shine at.

3. **Transparent dreaming.** As something that we grow out of doing the older we get, transparent dreaming takes intentional actions and prompting. By answering the question *With no judgment, no fears, and no limits, who do you want to be?* you get the opportunity to return to whatever age you were at where dreaming was appropriate, acceptable, and welcomed.

4. **Inspiration declaration.** The question *What deeply moves and motivates you* is your way to document how you garner your inspiration.

Let's explore all of the components of this Life Thesis deeper so that you can start making strides on your overall leadership legacy.

1. **Reflection of recurring events.** After doing the same things, traveling the same paths, and seeing the same people over and over and over again, day in and day out, it eventually puts us into autopilot. Think about the end of the year, when we often spend time reflecting on what we may have accomplished personally and even in the workplace.

   Think about when you start to document all of those small accomplishments and wins that you had all year. Are you shocked? Did you forget about that thing that you did in January that garnered so much support across your organization? Did you forget about that community initiative that you launched in your neighborhood and how well it was received? When we're on autopilot, we miss a lot of information, a lot of activities, and a lot of details. This is why we have to intentionally reflect. The very first component of the Life Thesis helps you to document and challenges you to reflect on the things that keep positively showing up in your life.

What are the things that you just can't shake (and you don't really want to) and they just keep showing back up for you?

For example, mine is public speaking. I started speaking on stages when I was in the fourth grade and although I spent my high school years and time in college trying to shake that off, it returned once again in my early 20s right as I was launching my first company. And quite honestly, public speaking has been a huge benefit both financially and also developmentally through-out my life. Public speaking and being on large stages are things that I can't shake and quite frankly, I don't want to anymore.

Other examples might include:

- As much as you try to pretend you're not a connector, you seem to always amass a plethora of people in your contacts, and it's always easy for you to see why these people should be connected and should know each other.

- Although you fully intend to lay low and not be the center of attention, somehow, someway, you naturally become the life of the party and people expect and appreciate that from you.

- Your memory does not fail you. You consistently recall the most detailed and complex details long after it's not even a faint memory in others' minds.

- You always seem to gravitate toward identifying the good in a situation or in a person no matter how dire, distressed, or catastrophic a situation is.

So what keeps positively showing up in your own life, no matter how hard you try to ignore it or pretend like it's not there?

2. **Assessment of your strong skills.** We all have strong skills. These are the things that we have either mastered or have just become really good at over time. Thinking about your strong skills can be tricky because, just as we go through life achieving things and then forgetting about them, sometimes we get really good at something and we start to believe that because we are so good at it, it's really not that big a deal. That is a corrupt approach. Your ability to be good at something, even if it's easy for you, now makes it even more important and essential. So take a second and think about your strong skills, the things that you know you are great at, and the things that serve you well in your life.

3. **Transparent dreaming.** Consider the question *With no judgment, no fears, and no limits, who do you want to be?* It's so easy when you're the tender age of five or six for you to answer, "What do you want to be when you grow up?" We encourage that behavior at a young age, but once you start approaching adulthood, we force ourselves to stop dreaming, to stop wishing, and to stop thinking about the things that we want to be in the spaces that we want to be in, personally and professionally. Well, I'm giving you permission again to consider, with no judgment, no fears, and no limits, who do you want to be?

   It's important to give yourself permission to think through that because it's not fair for us to stop dreaming at the age of 17. It's not fair for us to assume that just because we're headed off to college or our next phase in life and because we're creeping closer to age 21 and are probably able to drink alcohol legally, that instantly we should know everything and be who we're supposed to be for the rest of our lives.

Instead, we should lean into collectively developing more and more skills so that we can better refine our path, and more importantly arrive at a place where we can say, this is *one* of the things I want to do with my life.

So right now in this moment, I am giving you full permission to transparently dream. This isn't time for you to throw in words like "but" and "I can't" and "what about . . .?" I just want you to transparently dream.

4. **Inspiration declaration.** Every day isn't a magical day. In my life, many people around me think that I have good days every single day. Instead, my approach is that I have tools in place to quickly get me out of a mode that I don't want to operate in at that moment. I deeply value the importance of having tools that motivate and inspire me, especially at the moments when I need them the most.

So think about that for yourself. What deeply motivates and inspires you? It could be anything from reading a book to watching the sunrise to prayer and maybe even a nap. For me, I am very clear that business podcasts with a focus on people starting the things that they want to do motivate and inspire me. There's something about someone giving themself permission to go down a path to achieve things and to move to their next level that deeply fires me up.

It's one of the reasons why I launched the podcast *Just Start: From Ideas to Action,* which is deeply rooted in the storytelling of starting with nothing and turning it into something.

So for you, what is that thing or things? What is it that you can turn to when you're feeling your most depleted, when you're most unfulfilled, and you're most deenergized? What is that thing or who is that person that will give you a quick boost to get on the right path?

Now that we've explored the four core areas of your Life Thesis document, it's time to combine all those answers into one cohesive statement. This part of the exercise is essential, because this one statement can have the ability to help you make decisions in every component of your life. To provide some color into how this could work for you, I'm going to share my life thesis with you.

Jacqueline's Life Thesis: "My life will be a reflection of helping people just start the things that they want to do and elevate to their next level."

This simple yet profound statement helps me make decisions about the initiatives that I start, the things that I purchase on a day-to-day basis, the books I decide to write, the podcasts I decide to launch, and even the people who are actively allowed in my life. And it can do the same for you.

The Life Thesis is a part of your leadership legacy. It leans deeply into the self-leadership pillar of leadership levels. It also does something critical. It helps to identify your why. And as many of us know, the why of your life is the root of how you go about making other decisions in your life overall and especially on your leadership journey. Now let's take a moment to turn our attention to others and how you can create a leadership legacy that impacts others and shines bright in their lives as well.

Creating Impact for Others

Your leadership legacy can be hugely beneficial to other people around you. Since legacies aren't just magically manifested but are carefully curated, it's necessary to be intentional, outcome driven, and authentic in your engagements with others. Your ability to embrace these key things puts you on a path to show up in the lives of others and leaves a lasting impact that is your leadership legacy.

Let's explore these areas.

Intention. While there are things in your life that just happen, making a massive impact on others is something that you have to be intentional about. And when you think of intention, I want you to automatically think about creating space and time. Our calendars can easily get filled with all sorts of things. Prime example: think about the last time you cleaned out your inbox and a short while later you realized it was full again. Spaces in our life will consistently get filled up with whatever, based on anyone else's agenda.

Your job is to be intentional about the things you put or allow into your space and intentional about where you're directing your time and energy. For you to create a meaningful legacy, you have to hold the space to be impactful to other people. That means that if there is an hour or two that you have earmarked every week to specifically pour into and make yourself available to other people in whatever capacity it is that you sit in, it is your responsibility to do so. It could be done in informal and formal ways, but it does require a level of intent.

Outcome Driven. On your mission of creating meaningful impact in other people's lives, what are the results and outcomes that you are encouraging or helping them to achieve? When you hear the word "outcomes," your mind might gravitate more toward business-related subjects. But outcomes can mean a lot of different things. It could be someone recognizing that they just need to speak up a bit more. Or recognizing that there's an opportunity for them to advocate a bit more for themselves or even just embrace new things.

Being outcome driven with the people you permit in your sphere allows you to simply help them move the needle in their world. And that creates a substantial amount of impact in their lives. So while a casual conversation here and there with them is perfectly fine, are you committed to taking it further and actually driving toward outcomes and goals?

Authenticity. You are not a robot. Therefore, when you talk to people, when you share with them, and when you allow them into your world, it should be your job to adopt a spirit of transparency and authenticity. For people to best learn from you, to be able to absorb what you are sharing and apply it to their life, there needs to be a level of connectivity. And the best way to do that is to be authentic, to recognize that you are not perfect and hopefully no one is expecting you to be. What's most beneficial to others is understanding your path, understanding your insights, and sharing them to help them fill gaps in their journey to get to their next level. Embrace the power of authenticity and allow it to impact others around you.

Have you ever read or witnessed something that instantly stopped you in your tracks? Recently I ran across one simple statement that completely summed up my thoughts around leadership legacy:

Applause is temporary.

This statement is so profound to me because our minds have been programmed to think that "legacy" only means that you're physically leaving something for someone. And while that definition does apply, consider another connotation.

The creation of your leadership legacy and intentional work on it means that you will leave something planted inside of people, something that will continue to serve them over and over again and, more importantly, something that they're able to pass along to other people to be planted, nurtured, and reharvested inside them again and again. So, while active applause is temporary, the implanting of your leadership legacy on other people can be forever.

Now that we've discussed how creating your leadership legacy will be beneficial to you and to other people, it's time to actually identify both when you'll do that and—more immediately—how. I know you may be thinking, "That sounds great, but Jacqueline, how am I going to navigate this seemingly dense world of leadership, and when am

I actually going to find the time in what is already a busy life to activate any of these things"?

Before we dive into answering that question, let me first ask another. What is your preferred clothing style? If you think about how you'll dress over the next year, certain items of clothing might immediately come to mind. And while you'll likely have particular preferences, your answers might shift based on your situation, the location, and what the event is.

If you decided to take a moment to peruse your closet, you'd likely see a plethora of different clothing options. While there are some of your absolute favorites in there, you're probably not going to wear that evening gown or tuxedo every day of the week and to every event. You're going to be flexible, inquire about the dress code when applicable, and dress for the situation.

Just as clothing choices vary with situations, so do situations affect leadership choices, which is why it's in your best interest to switch up your leadership styles and remain flexible.

Let's dive into Chapter 5, where we'll explore the many leadership styles that you can select from, then we'll help you decide which one resonates most with you.

5 Leadership Styles

'd like you to think about the route you normally take from your home to your favorite grocery store. How long does it take? What are the typical landmarks along the way? How many stoplights do you typically pass?

Now, if for some reason the path that you normally travel was under construction, what alternate path would you take? There isn't just one way to get to your local grocery store. Based on how fast you want to get there, whether you want to take the scenic route, or if you feel like dealing with a certain number of stop signs or traffic lights, you may choose to go your typical route or deviate as you see fit. In other words, you have options! You can switch it up.

The routes you choose to take to the grocery store—or anywhere, for that matter—aren't the only situations in life where you have options to switch it up.

Think about how you used to handle issues or disagreements in your life 10–15 years ago. While many of us depend on our tried-and-true values, we've acquired a level of wisdom and experience that allow us to handle issues more eloquently and more effectively based on our experiences, education, and knowledge. It's also as a result of us

adopting different styles we can use to address various issues. Many of
us may just brush off our knowledge with passive comments like these:

- "I'm not the person I used to be."
- "A 20-year-old me would have."
- "I have a lot more to lose."

But the truth is that there is more to you than those passive
statements. You've in fact grown *and* adopted new ways to handle
situations. You've matured into someone who recognizes that there is
a different way to arrive at situations and you've elevated to an
operating mode where you're not just being reactive; you're addressing
situations in a manner that is productive, effective, and in line with
your true leadership potential.

This proves one very important thing: that you can change, you
can switch up your style to address situations in ways that are most
effective and that complement the outcome that you want to achieve.

You're on your way to fully embracing different leadership styles.

Now you may be wondering, *How can I just switch up my style?
Shouldn't my style be organic, pure, and authentic to me?*

And to that I say, absolutely!

But just as you have preferences about clothing choices, routes
that you take to get from point A to point B, and you switch up your
dinner selections to keep things interesting, you can flex, adjust, and
pivot based on the situation. You have the same opportunity to do so
with leadership.

Leadership Tip: *Don't get your wires crossed when thinking about
leadership styles. It's easy to think that your core values and leadership
styles are the same thing. Your core values are your fundamental beliefs
as a person. They should guide many of your decisions, including which
leadership styles you may or may not utilize in a situation.*

The Nine Leadership Styles

This chapter explores each of the nine leadership styles. I'm going to share with you not just the style, but my experience with each, along with some other nice-to-knows.

1. **Affiliative** leadership essentially puts people first. It focuses on creating a harmonious environment and explores how to build emotional bonds. This leadership style requires lots of understanding, empathy, and the ability to build relationships through a range of communication techniques and leadership styles employed by others. This style sounds almost magical, doesn't it? I mean, who doesn't want a "harmonious environment"? Historically, the types of people and organizations who do not embrace this style are traditional and conservative institutions and individuals who work hard to separate emotion from work. More recently, as organizations have become more open to discussing an employees' whole self and embracing more openness and transparency in the workplace, even from a personal standpoint, this style of leadership has become more popular and more widely adopted. In my most recent corporate role as the vice president of startup discovery at one of the nation's largest nonprofits, the affiliative leadership style was welcome and effective within our particular team. The startup feel of this particular job environment encouraged the development of relationships beyond just work, so this style of leadership was valued and was used often.

2. **Autocratic** leadership, also known as authoritarian leadership, is a style indicative of individual control over all decisions with little input from team members or others. Autocratic leaders typically make choices based on their own ideas and judgments and very rarely accept advice from followers. This style is generally frowned upon, although it is not uncommon to find it embraced by leaders at an organization, even unknowingly. Usually, autocratic

leadership is accompanied by a level of fear, where people are not empowered to disagree, to provide constructive criticism, or even to be remotely out of alignment with their leaders. Every one of my experiences working alongside autocratic leaders contained an unspoken level of dislike or lack of trust for the leader. While fear of retaliation kept this distrust from being voiced, the atmosphere eventually led to the top talent exiting the organization, largely because of the leader's style. This particular style of leadership outside of the workplace might show up in various ways professionally or even in friendship circles. And, while our lives are filled with different elements and scenarios that require dominance, direction, and guidance, the complete inability ever to listen to any feedback might be linked to some autocratic tendencies that may not serve you, serve the situation, or deliver acceptable outcomes.

3. **Coaching** is the leadership style that creates a culture of high performance. This style fosters collaboration, empowerment, and gratification. Coaching also incorporates mindsets and behaviors aimed at creating the highest performance opportunities for team members. Coaching continues to be one of the most effective leadership styles, but its success is highly dependent on both the leader coaching and also the subordinates' abilities and desire to be coached. If neither the coach nor the "coachee" is willing to assume their roles, it turns into an unwinnable situation. When I think about coaching, my mind gravitates toward some of the work I have the opportunity to do in the etiquette space with youth and adults. Because etiquette sometimes has an abrasive, rigid, and overly traditional feel to it, I choose to approach the subject in less of a lecture format and more from a coaching approach. If students are able to come to a conclusion about why they should be utilizing etiquette practices in their lives without having it drilled into them, it's a much more effective approach

and outcome. That is the power of coaching: asking the right questions and guiding people to their outcomes without dictating or lecturing.

4. **Democratic** leadership, also known as participative leadership or shared leadership, is a type of leadership style where members of a group take a more participative and active role in the decision-making process. This leadership style is common and can be quite effective. It supports an "all-in" approach where everyone has the opportunity to weigh in and have input on whatever issue or discussion is on the table. While this style has great team building and camaraderie benefits, it can also easily lead to an analysis paralysis dilemma, where there are so many options and potential avenues on the table that the group cannot make one finite decision. At some point, a decision has to be made and if a leader isn't able to distill the input voiced by the team into meaningful action, a situation can feel never-ending and overly analyzed. I have witnessed and used this style many times throughout my own leadership journey in my corporate role, within organizations that I have founded and even within my friend group as I was organizing social functions. The leader's ability to hear the input of others, while still understanding that an ultimate decision must be made, has been effective and successful. A big benefit to embracing this style is that you diminish any blind spots and unaddressed issues since there is more to it than just you curating all of the ideas, solutions, and insight. This style is widely accepted in many environments.

5. **Laissez-faire** leaders take an approach rooted in having trust and reliance on their team and the individuals around them. They don't micromanage or get too involved in minute details and don't give too much instruction or guidance. Instead, laissez-faire leaders let the individuals involved use their creativity, resources, and experience to help them meet their goals. While this style is

embraced in corporate settings, it tends to be more successful and appropriate at small or even startup-level organizations. For hierarchical organizations, there are multiple levels of reporting, and because it's expected for a leader to know what their subordinates are working on and accomplishing, this leadership style might make it harder to keep a pulse on real-time results. This style is common in noncorporate environments as well, but it still requires a high degree of trust by everyone involved. Personally, this is one of my favorite styles, particularly when I held a corporate role. I am the kind of team member who doesn't generally need a lot of direction or hand-holding, so for a leader to trust me completely and not expect minute-by-minute results, that was ideal for me. I did fully understand that it required me to make sure that I showed up and delivered results, and that I did not take undue advantage of the extreme autonomy that came along with this style of leadership.

6. **Pacesetting** is a style of leadership wherein a leader leads from the front. This style is one that constantly sets high standards for the team and expects them to exceed with minimal guidance or support. As a manager, you set the tempo for your team and demand high intensity in their performance. When you think of pacesetting, think of role-modeled behavior. This style is usually more visible and utilized in environments where tactical or physical work needs to be accomplished. While pacesetting leadership can be a value-added and effective style, if the leader modeling this behavior unrealistically seems to work 24/7/365 or expects results from their team that they themselves don't demonstrate are possible, they may be setting false and unsustainable patterns. Overall, however, this style is widely utilized and can be effective.

7. **Servant** leadership style is rooted in the idea that leaders should focus on serving the needs of the team. Servant leaders put the

needs of the people involved at the forefront. In this style, the team sees the leader as the central point of a team, but since the leader is deeply focused on the team's needs, there is a continuous cycle of development and achievement. At a first read, this style may sound very similar to the affiliative leadership style. The biggest difference is that the affiliative approach includes, welcomes, and fosters emotional bonds among team members. In affiliative, you may even hear a leader attempting to formulate "family-like" bonds. In the servant style, leaders are more focused on team member needs individually. This style is highly effective, and one that leaders are proud to embrace. While you won't often hear someone say that they are a pacesetting leader or an affiliative leader, you will in fact hear someone say that they are a servant leader.

8. **Transactional** leadership is a style in which leaders promote cooperation through both punishment and rewards. Through this style, transactional leaders are usually able to keep people motivated for the more immediate short-term. While not always effective due to its perception of fostering favoritism, this style is often used in many service scenarios where there are quotas and sales goals to be reached. This is a widely acceptable style of leadership but can often become ineffective because of the scorekeeping nature of the style, which isn't always motivating to many people.

9. **Transformational** leadership is where leaders motivate, inspire, and encourage employees to innovate and foster disruptive change that will help grow and shape the future success of their organization. This style is acceptable, but mostly when an organization is undergoing or needs to undergo a significant amount of change and disruption. From a corporate standpoint, transformational leaders are welcomed in and ultimately are the saving grace or reason for catapulted success. This was the case at

companies such as Best Buy, Ceridian, Apple, IBM, Microsoft, and Amazon. This style is highly effective when it's truly needed. A company that is constantly making monumental shifts and adjustments makes people nervous about the stability, reliability, and dependency of the organization. This style can also be effective in noncorporate settings as well when there might be a need to restructure, relaunch, or redirect a personal project, a community initiative, or even a family reunion or girls' trip that is headed off track.

Which of the nine leadership styles most resonates with you? If you have a hard time narrowing down to just one, that's not such a bad thing. Effective leaders actually embrace multiple styles depending on the situation. Since no two situations are alike, it will be continuously necessary to assess the situation and reference which style will help you get to the best possible outcome.

Do you find that you tend to embrace more than one style? Can you immediately think of a leader with whom you've worked with in the past who embraced a style above that makes you cringe, one that you found to be ineffective or inappropriate based on the situation?

Although some of the styles discussed above may not always be desired based on the situation, there is a scenario where each of them could have a very real and necessary role. While some of the styles may give people the warm fuzzies and may seem easier to embrace and own, let me remind you that as a leader, your role is not to always make the easy, warm, and fuzzy decisions. Sometimes there will be tough decisions that require collecting detailed feedback from each and every person, and sitting together in a kumbaya-style situation just won't work. Always remember that you have the opportunity to assess each situation that you are in independently and decide which leadership style you should embrace for the best possible outcome.

You will be able to assess the strengths and weaknesses of each style and make an informed decision on how best to proceed.

But before I dive into the pros and cons of each leadership style, let me address another pseudo style of leadership. When I say pseudo, I don't want to imply that it's not a real thing, but it's actually less of style and more of a mode of operation.

Situational Leadership® is a model created in 1969 by Paul Hersey and Ken Blanchard in their groundbreaking book *Management of Organizational Behavior*. It is an adaptive leadership approach that involves leaders taking stock of their team members, weighing each and every situation individually, and deciding which leadership style should be applied for that scenario.

Just as we choose which of the clothes in our closet make the most sense to wear based on what kind of event we're attending, choosing which leadership style to adopt depends on the particular situation. Yes, you may like tall heels or that custom tuxedo, but wearing that to a basketball game just doesn't make the most sense, right?

Situational Leadership is not a leadership style, but instead a state of being. It is the active process of committing to assessing a situation and applying the best style or styles. Remember when I previously asked if you tend to embrace multiple leadership styles? If you answered yes to that, you are already a steward and ally of the Situational Leadership model.

We also have choices on how we lead. The power of embracing Situational Leadership is that you have the option of expanding the way you lead by applying more than one leadership style to a situation.

Now let's take a look at the pros and cons of the nine leadership styles.

Leadership Style	What Is It	Advantages	Disadvantages
Affiliative	"People come first."	Can be motivating to individuals	Could cause a distraction to business goals
Autocratic	"Do as I say."	Can be majorly beneficial during crisis and chaos	Can be demotivating if always used
Coaching	"Give this a try."	Improves team performance, while addressing company goals	There is a great deal of autonomy for the person being coached. With autonomy comes a greater degree of free will and independence. In order for this style to be effective, the "coachee" has to take action and be willing to be coached and if they aren't willing to do so, this style isn't effective.
Democratic	"Let's decide."	Can foster a sense of shared accountability	Could cause too much needed buy-in for all things
Laissez-Faire	"What do you think?"	Highly effective when a staff is capable of managing themselves	Can't be used consistently because the need for your presence could be questioned

Leadership Style	What Is It	Advantages	Disadvantages
Pacesetting	"Keep going; let's make this happen."	Can be a great way to role-model behavior	Can be overwhelming if overused
Servant	"What can I do for you?"	Can instill a sense of loyalty from staff	The leader might be taken advantage of if not monitored accordingly.
Transactional	"I'll do this if you do that."	Competitive team members may find this attractive.	The risk and reward model may not always work or be a motivating factor for everyone.
Transformational	"Let's change things up."	Keeps a team at the forefront of what's new, trendy, and effective and improves efficiency	It can be unsettling without appropriate buy-in.

Now that you know you don't have to box yourself into a one-size-fits-all situation, let's discover how to find your default leadership style, while remaining flexible to embrace other styles when needed.

Finding Your Leadership Style

While embracing leadership styles as they are needed and most useful in a given situation is the most effective approach, there is still an advantage to understanding what your default style is. This is the style that you naturally gravitate toward. If you've ever taken a personality assessment, such as Myers-Briggs Type Indicator, DISC

personality assessment, Caliper Profile, or Eysenck Personality
Inventory, the goal is to get an understanding of who you are and
how you approach situations and conversations right now and
historically. This isn't to say that you aren't willing to adjust, elevate,
and grow, because you understand your natural tendencies and
personality. As a matter of fact, it's more beneficial if you do know
what your default is. It helps you to understand how you will react to
and tackle a situation without any mental intervention or shifts.

The same approach is true with your default leadership style.
Understanding where your default is prepares you to understand the
ease with which you might flex left, right, up, or down to other
leadership styles that best suit a situation. For example, if you are
naturally a servant leader and a situation requires you to be
significantly more direct and prescriptive so that a high visibility goal
is achieved, it may be necessary for you to temporarily embrace an
autocratic style.

So then, how do you discover what your default style is?

Your default leadership style is a combination of core components
that are already a part of your everyday world. While this book is a
guide to help you develop and elevate in your leadership journey, you
already bring some valuable things to the table by way of just being
who you naturally are. Let's explore some of those things as we home
in on your default leadership style.

The Leadership Wheel

The six-pronged Leadership Wheel in Figure 5.1 is designed to be
repetitive and ever evolving. While I want you to assess all six steps
and then move forward to determining your default leadership
style, you may elevate and change over time. (As a matter of fact,
I encourage you to!) This wheel encourages you once again to
navigate through the six steps and make another default leadership

style determination as you grow and change throughout your leadership journey.

Let's get you started on your first go round of the Leadership Wheel.

1. Outline Your Values

Your values are the priority factors that have the potential to guide your entire life. Think of them as your moral and ethical standards upon which the rest of your decisions lean. Understanding your values is incredibly important throughout your life. Actually, once you have them identified, it should make your life a bit easier, because

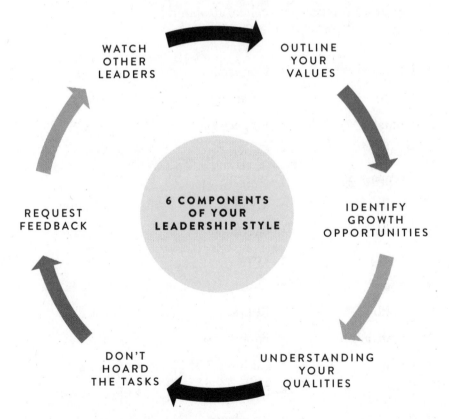

Figure 5.1 The Leadership Wheel.

these foundational priorities can guide both easy and complex decisions. For example, if making a difference is a fundamental priority for you and is a core value, you're probably going to prioritize and engage in activities that support that throughout the year.

Making a difference happens to be one of my core values, and remembering that greatly guides the way that I lead and the things that I choose to commit to. Although I never preclude myself from embracing any of the leadership styles previously presented, I know that I have a more natural inclination to the servant, coaching, and affiliative styles because their tangential connections make me feel like I am making a difference.

Take a moment and think about your top five values. While this list is far from comprehensive, here are a number of values for you to consider:

- Charisma
- Humor
- Courage
- Balance
- Compassion
- Family
- Freedom
- Security
- Loyalty
- Wealth
- Cooperation
- Clarity
- Fitness
- Relationship
- Connection
- Creativity
- Respect
- Generosity
- Integrity
- Wellness
- Gratitude
- Love
- Order
- Respect
- Forgiveness
- Faith
- Learning
- Excellence
- Innovation
- Wisdom
- Honesty
- Adventure
- Kindness
- Innovation
- Knowledge
- Patience
- Gratitude
- Fun
- Justice
- Abundance
- Reciprocity

2. Identify Growth Opportunities

I must be honest in saying that I have a love-hate relationship with the term "weakness," which is why you don't see it as a label header here. We're switching it up and embracing *growth opportunities*. This is because "weakness" has connotations of demeaning, belittling, and nonprogressive. Even one of your most haunting growth opportunities could potentially be a benefit in the right situation. But understanding what those opportunities are is still a value-added activity that will serve you, independent of whether you don't like that about yourself or it doesn't really bother you that much.

Where do you have the opportunity to grow?

3. Understand Your Qualities

There are things about us that just are. Sometimes we know why these things are and sometimes we have no clue where we picked up these quirks, habits, and qualities. Whether or not we know where we got them, it's essential that we acknowledge that they just are. Understanding our personality traits and qualities is one of the core foundational values to help us ultimately understand where we fall on the leadership style spectrum. What I mean by personality traits are those things that are germane and unique to you that make up who you are.

The good thing about personality traits is that there are so many of them and you likely possess at least several. We get so used to being "us" that we forget that we're made up of a lot of meaningful and valuable traits. Some of your qualities might include:

- Generosity
- Self-control
- Open-mindedness
- Persistence

- Optimism

- Sincerity

- Integrity

If you're stumbling over your thoughts at this moment trying to pin down what your personality traits are, there's another way to be introduced or reminded of them: through personality assessment tools.

Whether you're new to any of these tools or you're committed to revisiting them to see how far you've come in your development and leadership journey, from now on I want you to look at these tools differently. I want you to *take note* of your natural and organic approach to things, but be willing to adjust based on the leadership style that you need to embrace to get the results that you need in a particular situation.

Here are some of the most common personality trait assessment tools:

- Myers-Briggs Type Indicator

- DISC personality test

- Caliper Profile

- 16 Personality Factor Questionnaire

- Eysenck Personality Inventory

You don't have to take all five of these assessment tests. But I do encourage you to take one, two, or even three. And the results from these assessments should not give you permission just to say, "Well, this is who I am and the world will just have to deal with it." Instead, personality assessments should give you a benchmark of where you are and how you handle things based on how you approach things at that point in your life. Just because the test says that you generally approach things one way does not mean that you have to or will approach things this way forever. It gives you a snapshot of your mode of operation at that moment. It's up to you to continue to remember that you committed to an elevating leadership journey and that you have the ability to change. Just because you've been something, acted a certain way, or perhaps have been deficient in a particular area throughout your life doesn't mean that you have to continue to operate in that manner.

What are some core qualities that you recognize about yourself?

4. Don't Hoard the Tasks

Are you a task hoarder? Do you often believe that the only way X will get done correctly is if you do it? Do you cringe at the thought of someone else taking on and owning a task that you've so perfectly perfected and mastered? Well, I'll be the first to say that I do. I have historically had a hard time with sharing the work, sharing the tasks, and understanding the power of delegation. I know exactly where this behavior comes from. As a former wedding and event producer via my first company, Opal E Event Planning, I developed the necessary habit of being the point person consistently and, because we were in the business of wedding production, there was a strong emphasis on making sure that things went right all the time.

But there's another consideration when you're a task hoarder, and that is that you miss out on two opportunities:

1. Freeing up your time to develop yourself and to give yourself permission to do the next thing that you're supposed to master
2. Providing someone else with the opportunity to execute that task, master that task, and move on to their next level of leadership as well

Delegation isn't a punishment; delegation is an opportunity. And as much as we begin believing that the way that we specifically do a task may be the best and only way to do it, the reality is there are a million different ways to get one thing done. Just like there are a million different ways for us to drive a route from our workplace to home or from a shopping trip to home, it is true that there are other ways for things to get done than just the way that you do them. So remember to leave space in your life to delegate, not just for the sake of your own leadership journey but also for the sake of others as well. As you're thinking about your default leadership style and which one most resonates with you based on how you tend to handle delegation, ask yourself:

Do I have the ability to delegate and share ownership of tasks/responsibilities?

5. Request Feedback

Have you ever experienced being around a child who continuously asks questions? "Why is that?" and "What did you think about that?" and "How did you do that?"

Most kids have no problem bombarding you with questions, waiting for the answers, and consistently demanding feedback. But at some point in our lives we stop soliciting feedback. We go into this mode of pretending that we know everything, so asking questions and soliciting feedback just isn't necessary. But it's a mistake! Feedback is the single largest way to learn about ourselves.

From imposter syndrome (the suspicion that you don't really deserve the position or respect that you've achieved in life) to body dysmorphia (a mental health disorder in which you can't stop thinking about one or more perceived defects or flaws in your appearance), sometimes we need a bit of outside support and input to help us see the full view of our ourselves, not just the one that we make up or think is true from our own perspectives.

Feedback can come from a number of sources, both personally and professionally. I want you to get quality feedback that you can take action on and that is meaningful. If you're just out to collect cheerleaders who are going to say only what you want to hear, this is not that. The goal here is to understand more about yourself so that you can better decide what leadership style you most align with. When soliciting for feedback, embrace these steps:

- **Tell them why you want the feedback.** "I'm working on refining my leadership skills, so I'd like to get feedback on your experiences with me to better inform my development opportunities."

- **Let them know you want the truth.** Some people feel compelled to sugarcoat things and wrap them up in a bow. While people don't have to be nasty and rude when giving feedback, it is important that they are honest, so that you can actually take action. You can say, "I'm really looking for your candid, honest feedback here."

- **Ask clarifying questions.** Sometimes people need more than one opportunity to say what they're trying to say. Say things like, "Can you tell me a bit more about that?" or "An example or two of when I may have done that would be helpful."

- **Document it.** We often have the best intentions of remembering everything that someone said, and then we don't. While getting valuable feedback, don't trust your memory to do what it has failed to do so many times. Write down what the person is saying or, if they're comfortable with it, record it. *Many people may not be comfortable with being recorded, so don't be offended if someone opts to not want to go this route.* ***Be prepared to take notes instead.***

- **Stay judgment free.** Remember that we often see ourselves differently than how other people see us, so when someone gives us feedback, it may not be what we expected them to say. While soliciting and receiving feedback, it's in our best interest to commit to being a student learning about yourself from the eyes of others. This isn't the time to be defensive, try to plead your case, or engage in a rebuttal. Feedback given to you doesn't mean that you have to change everything about yourself immediately. It just gives you data points and insight so you can collectively assess the pieces and understand more about you.

When was the last time you solicited honest feedback from someone you trust? Were you able to digest the feedback and take action on it? Did you find yourself not wanting to believe the feedback, or questioning it?

6. Watch Other Leaders

There are meaningful leadership activities happening around us all the time. And they're not just happening in the workplace; they're happening in our social and personal lives as well. It's up to us to pull our head out of the sand and pay attention to those examples. When I say observe your leaders, even in *unexpected places*, consider this:

- These might be your neighbors who selflessly head out to pick up trash in the neighborhood when they're never compensated for that.

- It might be your fellow PTA member who goes above and beyond to ensure that everyone on the PTA receives some small token of appreciation for holidays that many people don't even celebrate.

- It could be the hostess at the restaurant that you frequent, who you witness advocating for accessibility-friendly restaurant menus so that all guests can have a sense of independence while dining there.

It's easy for us to adopt a practice of watching leadership occur from the sidelines, but never "request" to be taken off the bench. Observe the people around you who are making meaningful unexpected leadership waves both inside and outside the workplace. You'll probably find that these people are flexible in their styles as well, sometimes unknowingly. While there is a natural style that they may gravitate toward, they likely recognize that in order to be a reliable, meaningful, and relevant leader, they need to be flexible. Observe their actions and utilize them to better help you decide where you are on the leadership style spectrum and where you can be flexible and nimble.

What have you observed from other leaders to assess their style and approach?

Determining your leadership style is an essential step in your leadership elevation journey. The exciting part of developing your style is that you're not stuck with it. You can understand which style(s) you are most comfortable with and gravitate toward, but also give yourself permission to flex and adjust when the situation warrants it. Also, understanding that there is a catalog of different leadership style opportunities gives you the flexibility to revisit that list of styles and decide which option you should veer toward for different scenarios you encounter. There'll be times where being democratic is an essential part of being a leader and there'll be times where you have to be incredibly definitive and direct. Neither of those styles are wrong, but there's a time and a place and an application for both of them.

Also, you may look at the list of leadership style options and recognize that you consistently embody multiple styles. This is incredibly common. And it's actually a great start for you. I want you to be fluid in your approach to leadership and adopt the Situational Leadership method, especially if you're already straddling two or more styles.

Resist the urge to feel like that's not the right thing to do and that true leaders stay consistent with one style. There are no two situations, two people, or two challenges that are exactly the same, so it wouldn't serve you or anyone else to try to resolve everything with the same approach and style.

Give yourself permission to be flexible.

Now that we've explored the different leadership styles and you've taken a spin of the Leadership Wheel, which style do you think is your default style?

II Leadership Elevation

We've spent the first five chapters setting the needed groundwork and unveiling what to expect while you're on the leadership journey.

Now, let's take it a step further.

Let's refine your skills and dive into the six leadership areas to explore as you elevate. In this next section, you will be challenged and encouraged to embrace new thinking, shed old practices, and fully step into your leadership opportunities.

Let's keep going!

6 Finding the Time to Refine

"'m fine" is the single most common response when someone asks someone else how they have been. Even when the person who was asked has been doing tremendously well or awfully bad, the most common response is still "I'm fine."

Now, why is that? Why do we say "I'm fine" even in moments when we're nowhere close to fine. Well, this could be for a myriad of reasons, including avoiding feelings, avoiding conflict, avoiding our problems, being overly modest, or not wanting to be disruptive in a passive environment.

It's also because our lives can easily drift into autopilot mode if we let them, and saying, "I'm fine" turns into one of those automatic responses that are easy and often mindless.

Let me give you the most common and obvious example of our lives on autopilot.

You've had a long day at work. All of the perfectly laid plans and meetings that you mapped out somehow decided to get a mind of their own and either run late or completely fall off track altogether. When the workday is complete, you gladly hop into your vehicle or jump aboard your daily public transportation knowing that every dollar you made that day, you earned. Almost instantly, you're exiting your transportation and heading toward your home door. As you reach for the doorknob, you quickly realize that your entire ride home was a complete blur. Although your commute is more than a hop and a skip from your workplace, you can't remember any of the details, including stop signs, stoplights, entering and exiting co-riders, the announcement of train or bus stops, the unrelenting honking of impatient drivers, or even the irritable neighboring toddlers. You went into autopilot mode and, like magic, you completely missed an entire hour of your life.

And, if we really think about it, we realize it happens a lot. Once we've done a task or activity a number of times, it becomes something that we can do without thinking very much about it all. The mere fact that we have 168 hours in a week and most of us can't remotely figure out where it all goes is proof enough that no one is siphoning our time from us. We are in fact allowing it to flow out of our lives on our own with our permission, by living a life on autopilot.

Recognizing the Risks of Autopilot

Do you operate on autopilot? Here are a few signs that you just might be on the autopilot wheel:

- You do the exact same tasks every day with no flexibility to adjust or change.
- You find that you arrive at certain places and you have no idea how you got there or you can't recall landmarks, activities, or actions.
- You can't fathom where the 168 hours of your week went to.

While autopilot operations may get you through the day, this ultimately does something far more damaging: it robs you of your moments. This is because some of the things that you've put on autopilot may no longer be serving you, may not be necessary, or may not even serve a purpose at all anymore. But, because you've put these things on auto mode and you keep doing them the same way over and over and over again, you're not giving yourself the opportunity to assess if you need to keep doing it that way, or doing it at all anymore.

Let's revisit the commuting example and I'll go into the lion's den this time for the sake of bringing this situation further to life. Not long ago, I hitched a ride to the airport with a dear friend of mine. Unlike most times when I drive myself to the airport, here I was riding in the passenger seat, so I had the option of being far more observant than normal. I noticed that my friend was taking a much different route than I would have taken, and it was actually taking a lot less time. She was using the navigation app Waze, which I had heard of but had yet to try it out. Instead, I drove to the airport the exact same way every single time, whether that way took me 25 minutes (a record!) or a whopping 60-plus minutes due to the infuriating Washington, DC, traffic. Instead of embracing this (not so new) tool that had been proven to work for my friend and many other people I knew, I had been operating on autopilot, doing the same thing over and over again because it was what I was comfortable with.

But that's dangerous.

Putting our life on autopilot is not smart or safe. Our personal and professional lives are always one quick moment away from having a significant change and if we're in autopilot mode rather than being aware or alert, we're not preparing ourselves to embrace what's always around the corner: change. When we subject ourselves to believing that change isn't going to happen and we're coasting on autopilot, we're setting ourselves up for failure, because change is constant and it's coming.

I laid all of this groundwork out in this chapter for one thing—to get you ready to deprogram yourself out of this cycle of just doing for the sake of doing and escape the haze of autopilot.

On this journey of leadership, it will be necessary both to declare your commitment to it, while also seeking out opportunities to refine. When I say seeking out opportunities, I want you to know that there are many options to do so. When we think about growing in our leadership journey, our minds may automatically drift toward certifications and degrees and advanced degrees. And, while those are surely options, there are ways to grow in your leadership journey that are far less expensive, considerably more accessible, and take significantly less time. Now, to be clear, this is not me saying that you don't need certifications and degrees. What I am saying is that I don't expect that you'll be taking a class or certification every time you need to advance in your journey. I'm not expecting you to shell out hundreds or thousands of dollars every week to learn or refine a new skill. I'm asking you to embrace the idea that learning opportunities are around us every day and sometimes it is a matter of shaking ourselves out of the automation of our lives so we can use our everyday experiences to grow in our leadership journey.

So where can you find this "alleged" time that you have?

Five Tools to Refine Your Inner Leader

I recognize that counting someone else's time can be dangerous. It might even be akin to trying to count someone else's money. And, since we're only six chapters into our newfound relationship, I'm going to tread lightly on potentially offensive activities. However, I will provide you five tools to work with as you're mapping out the time you need to define and refine your inner leader.

1. **Know what kind of learner you are.** Sometimes we go on this path of believing that we are incapable of retaining certain types of knowledge because of how it is presented to us. I clearly remember feeling incredibly incompetent about math when I was in high school. I spent a significant number of years thinking that math was just something I would never be good at. But later I realized it wasn't the math itself that I was bad at absorbing, but the mechanism and the method by which I was being taught. Later in life, I learned that I am mostly an auditory learner. It's one of the reasons why I so deeply love podcasts because I'm able to listen and absorb information that way and apply it toward my own personal situations.

Take a second to think about how you like to learn. Do you physically like to read a book? Do you prefer audio options or are you a tactile learner who needs to physically touch things in order to learn them best? By leaning into and being committed to learning how you learn best, you'll be able to put some tools in place to allow you to learn within the capacity of how you're already living your life. For example, on your commute home, whether you are in the car or on public transportation, you can use that time to listen to things. If you know for sure that you are an auditory learner or if you just want to explore whether that style of learning suits you, maximize your time within the confines of doing something that you were going to do anyway—travel home—and also listen to articles, books, and even podcasts that deeply lean into leadership topics you might want to refine.

One of the best ways to dig into discovering what type of learner you are is by doing. Give yourself permission to experiment. Try a book, try an article, try an audiobook or a podcast, try taking an actual class of some sort. But recognize that within the world that you're already in and within a task that you're already completing, you have the opportunity to learn a little bit more about yourself and utilize that time wisely.

There are four primary learning styles:

- *Auditory.* Sometimes referred to as the aural style, this is where the learner prefers to absorb content via voice.

- *Kinesthetic* learners like to learn by doing. They are drawn to opportunities to learn by touching and physically interacting.

- *Reading/Writing.* This type of learning style most resonates with people who prefer written information via reports, spreadsheet, and other documents.

- *Visual.* Visual learners better retain information that is presented to them via graphs, charts, symbols, diagrams, and pictures.

Which style of learner are you?

2. **Plan ahead.** If left to its own devices, our schedule gets packed each week. Someone else will conveniently plop some commitments into our life whether we want them to or not. It is your responsibility to prioritize the time you need. So, if that means that you're looking ahead 60 to 90 days just to block off an hour or two a week for your own personal development opportunities, do so. I know things always pop up unexpectedly and there are always competing commitments and expectations, but your job is to manage your time—all 168 hours that you get weekly. And if you think about it, out of that large block of time that we all have to work with every week, you deserve one to two hours a week specifically for yourself and your development opportunities.

Another approach to take in planning ahead is to separate yourself from your environment. If you know that you are prone to succumb to social media distractions, a needy child, or a talkative friend or family member—all items that could derail you from utilizing the time that you allocate for leadership refinement—it may be time for you to separate yourself from your normal environment. If you have the option of completely getting away for a single or even multiday personal retreat to focus on your development, do that, but I recognize that sometimes getting away for extended periods is quite the challenge, especially if you have small children, if you're caregiving for parents or grandparents, or if you're an integral part of your family and you haven't yet delegated key components. Try some of these shorter options to define your inner leader:

- Spend two hours in your local coffee shop reading up on a new skill.
- Wake up an hour before your family and read an article on leadership styles.
- Use 40 minutes of your lunch break to watch a video on public speaking skills.
- On Sunday evening, send out a survey to get feedback from some past colleagues on your leadership style.

Planning ahead for these items is the key to getting them done. If you're all excited about going to your coffee shop to read but you haven't planned for it and it's not something you normally do, you may lose steam if you run across even the most solvable roadblock. Take the time to plan out your learning activities well in advance.

3. **Lunch and learn.** If you work in a corporate environment, you likely have access to some type of training and learning portal with different courses you probably haven't even taken a look at. Although many of these courses could use a refresh, many can actually be incredibly suitable and beneficial. So the next time

you see a lunch and learn opportunity pop up in your workplace or even just an online leadership webinar of some sort, take a second and check it out. Because while I do encourage you to check out of work to take your lunch breaks, it may be beneficial every now and then for you to consume your lunch and also absorb some relevant and impactful leadership content at the same time.

Similarly, there are spaces to learn independent of the formal work environment. A quick scroll of any of my social media timelines always reveals some kind of webinar, live training, or article. As much as your autopilot mode may kick in to save you from junk posts, commit to being the leader who still keeps an eye out for the opportunity to learn your next leadership skill from an unexpected source.

4. **Task and activity audit.** We can be creatures of habit. And while habits can serve us well, habits can also unknowingly punish us. Think about an organization or a group that you've been a part of for a substantial amount of time. While that group may have served you at some point and you have had the opportunity to serve it, it is our responsibility to assess whether that organization or activity continues to play a role in our lives today. This is the perfect time to do a task and activity audit. Are the things that you are committed to and engaging in still meaningful to you?

   Is it time for you to pass the torch? You may decide that you're not ready to completely give up an organization or a commitment altogether, but consider that committee that you've been heading up now for years. Is it time for some fresh new talent to infuse some innovation and perhaps some energy into it because you're no longer interested or deeply committed? I want you to be honest at this moment and ask yourself, "Might I be able to free up a substantial amount of time in my life by being honest about the fact that I am no longer interested in that task or activity?"

This one small action could free up hours, days, weeks, or even months that you could utilize on other activities or even on your leadership development journey.

5. **You are important enough to be prioritized.** Isn't it fascinating that so many things around us can be essential and important and somehow we allow ourselves to be deprioritized in the process? You are important. Your goals are important. Your leadership development is important. And it'll be up to you for the rest of your life to remind yourself and the people around you of that. So when you consider taking that class off of your calendar—the one that you've been waiting to take for years—because something else requires your attention, I want you to first ask yourself, "Do I deserve this and do I need this?" Do you need this not just for the benefit of your leadership journey but also for others whom you'll impact along the way? You and your desires and your development are important enough to be prioritized.

I do understand that finding the time to do the things that we really want to do can be difficult. And it's difficult because there are other things around us that are continually competing for our attention. As you go deeper into committing to your leadership development, remember that you own your time. Your time doesn't own you. And while yes, we have commitments that fuel our life and allow us to have the resources to pay our bills and feed our family and clothe ourselves, we still have a level of autonomy over how we spend our time. My desire for you is that you earmark the time that you need to grow, develop, and elevate.

7 Your Leadership Blueprint

Have you ever looked at a real blueprint? I imagine that you may conceptually know what a blueprint is and you may even recall that, historically, blueprints were blue. But have you ever actually picked one up or even seen one lately? Things change and advance with time and blueprints are one of them because they aren't actually blue anymore. Before I get into why we're talking about blueprints in the first place, I want you to simmer on this notion for just a moment.

Blueprints were actually blue when they were created in 1842 by John Herschel, a polymath in science-related fields, but that changed in the 1940s, when less expensive printing methods and digital displays became available. Even though they aren't blue anymore, to this day many of us still refer to them as blueprints and would bet that they're actually blue. But the practitioners who actually utilize these documents no longer call them blueprints; they refer to them as drawings, prints, or plans. Nonetheless, it is still common to refer to these plans as blueprints.

I liken the concept of blueprints to help understand our relationship with leadership. A blueprint is a view of a structure or building at the core foundational level. This level is so important because when all of the decorative options get piled on top of the foundation, it has to be able to withstand and endure. When we talk about leadership, think of it as a bottom-up pyramid approach, but what you see at the top of the triangle may be a little different than what you may expect.

Understanding the Leadership Pyramid

We've already seen another version of our leadership levels in a circular format (Figure 5.1), but conceptualizing this as a pyramid (see Figure 7.1) helps you to further understand why your self-leadership journey is so essential.

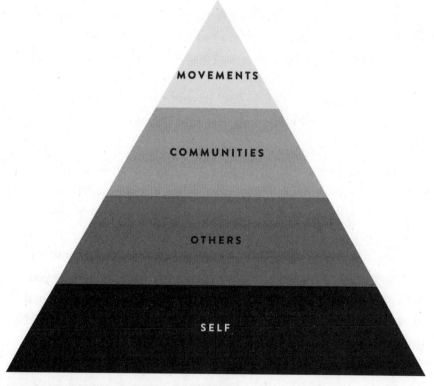

Figure 7.1 The Leadership Pyramid.

As the everyday leader that you are, you are responsible for ensuring that your self-leadership is sound, solid, and stable enough so that when you begin to elevate in your journey and add on other levels of leadership, your self-leadership foundation is still sound, uninterrupted, and supportive of where you want to go next. This is a similar concept to Maslow's Hierarchy of Needs, where the bottom tier of the pyramid is the foundation needed for the higher levels to be actualized. In Maslow's Hierarchy of Needs, that bottom level represents physiological needs, including breathing, food, water, shelter, clothing, and sleep. When those foundational needs are met, the other levels consisting of safety and security, loving and belonging, self-esteem and self-actualization can be more efficiently achieved.

There is a similar approach with the Leadership Pyramid. When the foundation of your leadership journey—self-leadership—is prioritized, nurtured, and committed to, when it's time to lead other people, to lead communities, and to lead movements, you're able to be more effective and confident.

Although there was a time when leadership was hugely focused only on a top-down approach, where you are continuously looking for someone to lead and direct you for you to advance, leadership has evolved into not just the process of leading others, but the importance of leading ourselves as well. This is the perfect time to remind you that things evolve, and so should you.

Why the Blueprint Matters

Back to the blueprint conversation. When was the last time that you looked at the components of a blueprint? Figure 7.2 shows the actual schematic blueprint of Skinphorea Facial Bar & Acne Clinic in metro Detroit. A blueprint is designed to provide you with the tactical steps that you might need to put something together. This something usually consists of a massive structure like a commercial building or a house.

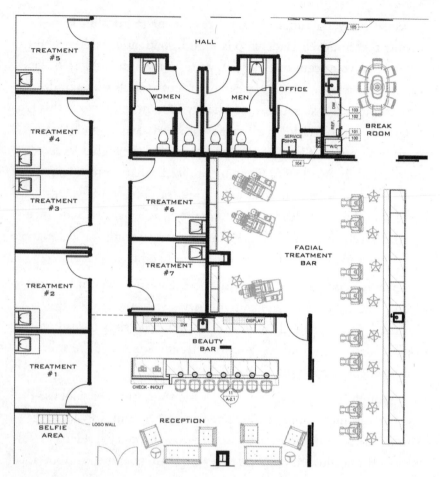

Figure 7.2 Skinphorea Facial Bar blueprint.

The whole idea of a blueprint is that the upfront planning is done to ensure that there is a plan to follow to make the construction, maintenance, and future renovations of the structure easier.

Ideally, this is a fantastic idea. Who doesn't want a guide, a structure, and a framework to ensure that whatever you're working on or climbing toward has been thought through, planned for, and mapped out?

Well, this is a perfect time for us to create the structure for your leadership journey. It's time for you to put together your very own blueprint, so that when you feel a little lost, a little unsure of yourself, or a little outside your leadership element, you have something to refer to, to help you feel directed, guided, and on track. A leadership blueprint is important for the times you come across scenarios different from what you're used to.

For example, how you lead yourself, how you lead other people, how you lead communities, and how you lead an entire organization may be in deep contrast with how you lead in coordinating the girls' trip or even how you lead in coordinating your family trips. In all these situations you'll be projecting leadership, but with slightly different approaches.

Your leadership blueprint sets the foundational components that won't change from situation to situation, but it allows you to take into account changing variables that will need to be adjusted for as you elevate deeper in your leadership journey.

We already took the time in Chapter 4 to dig deep into your leadership legacy. This was essential because you now have a long-term view of what you want your life's work to reflect. With that already documented and in place, you now have the opportunity to ensure that the way that you approach every unique situation contributes to that and supports that leadership legacy.

Having identified your leadership legacy, you should feel good about where you're at right now.

Leadership Tip: With life's eventual changes, you can always edit your leadership blueprint. Things like a new job, a new baby or family member, or even a new perspective on life might prompt this change and reevaluation.

The Elements of the Leadership Blueprint

Now, let's move on to understanding the specifics of your leadership blueprint so you can use it when it's needed. I am detailing the components of this so you can see and understand all the pieces, but as you begin to consistently utilize it, you'll likely need to refer to it less and less. It'll become second nature to think through the steps quickly to arrive at what your individual blueprint for that situation needs to be.

There are eight components of the Leadership Blueprint (Figure 7.3), which we will explore in detail:

1. Your values

2. The situation

3. Your desired outcome

4. Personal skill assessment

5. Team skill assessment

6. People involved

7. Leadership style needed

8. Alternate leadership styles needed

- **Values.** Luckily, we aren't new to the world of values, since we spent some time exploring them in Chapter 5 as we navigated our leadership styles. While we might hear the word "values" all of the time, most people aren't really clear about what a value is and what is its place in your life. Your values are your principles or standards of behavior and a judgment of what is important in life.

  Your values are likely constant. While there may be life-changing moments where a value could be removed or added, it's typically not something that you're willing to or should change every other week. Take a moment and reflect or remind yourself what your top five values are and remember that those are a priority to acknowledge as part of your leadership blueprint and journey.

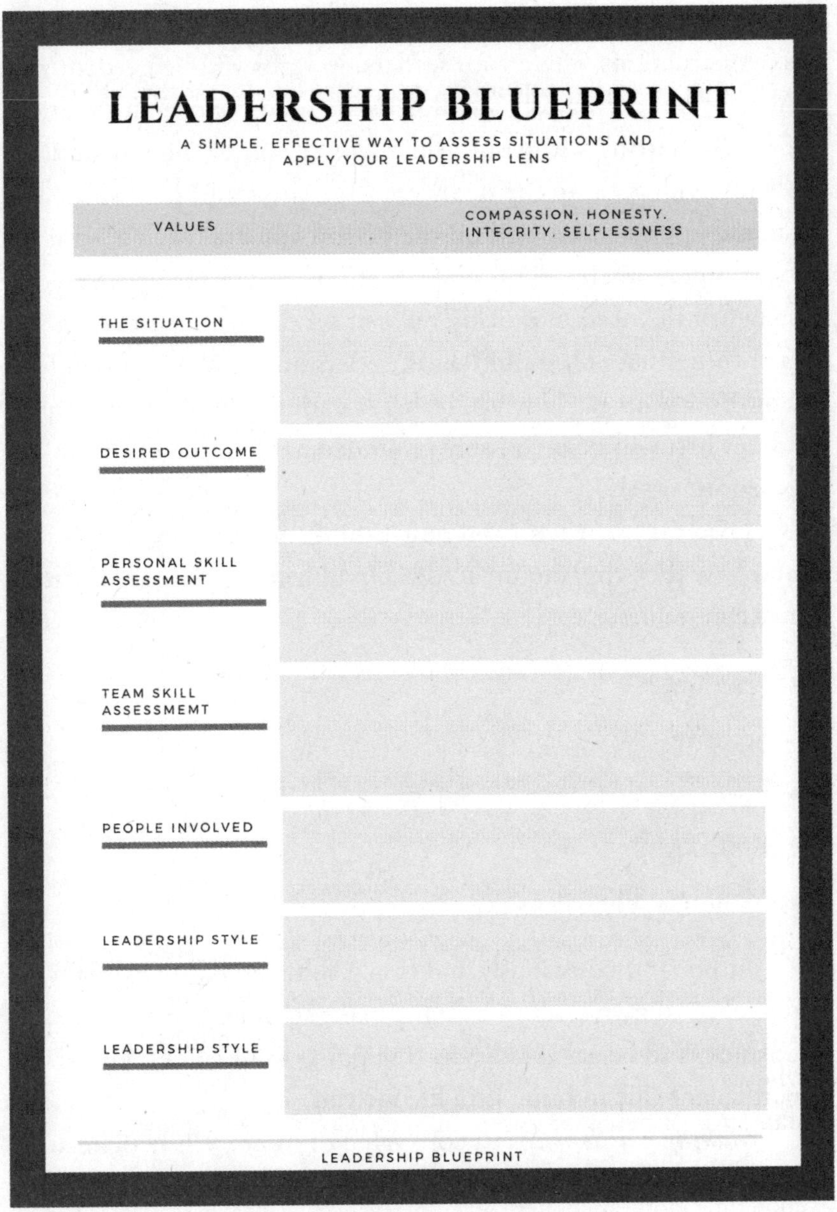

LEADERSHIP BLUEPRINT

A SIMPLE, EFFECTIVE WAY TO ASSESS SITUATIONS AND
APPLY YOUR LEADERSHIP LENS

VALUES	COMPASSION, HONESTY, INTEGRITY, SELFLESSNESS
THE SITUATION	
DESIRED OUTCOME	
PERSONAL SKILL ASSESSMENT	
TEAM SKILL ASSESSMEMT	
PEOPLE INVOLVED	
LEADERSHIP STYLE	
LEADERSHIP STYLE	

LEADERSHIP BLUEPRINT

Figure 7.3 The Leadership Blueprint.

Since this leadership blueprint will be used to help you assess situations where your leadership skills will be needed, you may be wondering why we didn't start with the overall situation first. By starting with your values, you're able to quickly decide (before you get into the nuances of the situation) how you should approach it based on the person you are (or you want to be) foundationally. With new situations and challenges, you may feel the need to quickly react or take action. Instead, the first thing that you should do is understand, "Who am I and how do I want to show up in this situation?" Identifying your values first will help you stay grounded and choose your reactions wisely.

I want to share with you how I think about my own values and how they apply to my leadership blueprint. Here are my top five core values:

- Freedom
- Security
- Love
- Reciprocity
- Making a difference

Although I consciously and (now) subconsciously mentally reference all my values to help me make sound decisions, get unstuck, and be a sound leader, I'm going to highlight one particular value to bring it to life for you.

Making a difference is a core value of mine. While there are many things that I can do in my life, and more specifically on my leadership journey, I feel most fulfilled and most valuable when I know that my actions are making a difference. If I apply this to people who I support on their leadership journey, I have to ask some questions to know if it's truly making a difference:

◆ How can I be helpful?

◆ Was that helpful?

◆ Was that insight helpful?

◆ Are there other challenges that you're facing that I can assist with?

◆ What can I take off of your plate or assist with?

◆ Do you have any blind spots that I can help with?

These and other questions will allow me to assist someone else, while at the same time to satisfy one of my core values. Although at that moment my attention is squarely on someone else and assisting, I am also getting something out of the situation as well—the satisfaction of one of my core values. By having core values in place, you create perpetual wins for yourself by both getting what you need and helping other people elevate at the same time.

• **Situation.** Now it's time to get specific. You'll encounter lots of different situations that require you to be fully aware of your leadership opportunities and impact. As you're acknowledging the situation that you're in, take a moment to document it. Be as specific as possible so that you can make an informed analysis of what to do next.

   While there are a lot of different situations, I'd like to offer a couple of examples to get you to see how you might document situations of your own:

   ◆ You have to have a difficult conversation with a direct report about their time management skills. You are incredibly unenthused about this conversation because this has been an ongoing issue for quite some time. You have an opportunity to lead with empathy, but also to be direct, action-seeking, and behavior-modification driven.

♦ You are the co-lead for your organization's women's affinity group and you want to ask a senior leader to give remarks at an upcoming event. Although you are thrilled about your leadership role in this group, you are reluctant to ask a senior leader to get involved since there does not appear to be widespread support for the initiative.

♦ You are nervous about leading the team meeting as a self-leader because you haven't had the opportunity to do so before.

♦ You signed up to be the core lead for your community's spring fling event. While this is a marquis event that everyone looks forward to, you're finding that no one else who signed up is taking their roles seriously, so all of the responsibilities are falling back on you.

• **Desired outcome.** Document what the most desirable outcome is for you. While it might feel overwhelming to write this down, especially if you're unsure of how you're going to get there, it's important to document this. The whole purpose of this exercise is to help you take a look at all the pieces in a particular situation and determine how you're going to get to the desired outcome. But if you are unclear about what the desired outcome is, it's difficult to get there. Yes, you may end up with this desired outcome or some version of it, but you have to start somewhere. So go ahead and document your desired outcome. Some examples might be:

♦ Launch a new product with the help of five team members

♦ Arrive at a solution for three team members to work from home while meeting business goals

♦ Personally take on a new work project while also working on other assignments

♦ Successfully serve as the chair for my upcoming family reunion

If you just jump into a situation with no plan, no "blueprint," and no approach, you could be spinning your wheels and wasting your time. Document your desired outcome so you can get to where you want to be faster.

- **Personal skill assessment.** Now it's time to look inward. While you've accomplished a lot and have a lot to be proud of, we are not all-knowing beings. The personal skill assessment is the time for you to document the key skills that are needed that you already possess to solve this situation. This is also a time for you to be transparent about the skills that you don't have that you can either learn or leverage from other people on your team or within your social circles to fill in the gaps. Imagine that you've been nominated to plan the upcoming family reunion and you're ready to accept the nomination and step up to the plate. There's this part of you that knows that while you can inspire others and get other key people on board, and that you are confident with being able to secure some vendors, you know that there are a multitude of other tasks that need to be done that just aren't your thing. You may even be able to specifically pinpoint that emceeing an event isn't something that you have experience doing or that you're comfortable with. This doesn't mean that you just opt out of the opportunity altogether. You just make note of what the skills are that you have and don't have so that you can plug the skill gaps.

This family reunion example actually makes me revisit the year 2019. This is when my husband was sorta "volun-told" that he would be chairing his 100-plus-person family reunion, which was slated to take place in Baltimore, Maryland. My husband has the unique ability to get people excited about initiatives, get a meaningful amount of buy-in from key family members, and has some level of emceeing skills. Now, where he has some gaps is absolutely in the event-planning area. But guess who spent eight years owning and operating an event management company? His wife, aka me. So, although he took the assignment knowing that he has some skill gaps, he knew that relying on some key team family members (like me) was an option.

- **Team skill assessment.** The team skill assessment is critical because it allows you to see overall what skills are at your and your teams' disposal, and it also helps you to quickly see if any of the gaps can be fulfilled by someone else on the team. Taking a team skill assessment can be done several different ways:

  - Assessing the knowledge that you have about team members
  - Inquiring with team members about their capabilities
  - Talking with people outside of the team about what they've observed or know about your team members

    This third option is important because sometimes people are modest about what they're capable of unless it's recognized by someone else. A simple highlight of their hidden skill set and an endorsement by someone else could be what you and the other person need to bring their skills to the surface.

    Also, I'd like for you to think more expansively about the word "team." In this context it isn't meant to reference only work team members. It is a representation of any group of people with whom you may engage to get things done. So this could be a friend group, family, sorority sisters, fraternity brothers, classmates, or fellow church members.

- **People involved.** If there are other people involved in the situation who are actively going to contribute to your desired outcome, it's time to document those individuals. These people might be advisors, vendors, or a number of other roles. By being clear that there are other resources, you can set expectations with your team so they recognize that there is additional support or potential consensus required from these people.

- **Leadership style needed.** There are nine distinct leadership styles that you can choose to utilize (see Chapter 5 if you need a refresher). While you may gravitate toward an organic leadership style, there are several other styles that you have the opportunity to adopt given the situation of your blueprint. So, in thinking through this particular situation, what leadership style do you feel will be the most relevant and the most helpful to apply to get your desired outcome? Understand what it is and document it on your leadership blueprint.

  If you need to have a high degree of buy-in and consensus in this situation, you may choose to adopt a democratic leadership style as the best option. If you know that this is a situation where a resolution and outcomes are needed fast and that the team needs specific directions and guidance on how to get through a situation, you may need to temporarily adopt an autocratic style.

- **Other leadership styles needed.** Depending on how complex your particular situation is, it may be necessary for you to adopt multiple leadership styles. You may have to start out utilizing one style and then gravitate toward another to wrap this up and bring it home. So is a second leadership style needed? Add it to your blueprint.

Now is the perfect time to remind you that leadership is an art and not a science. And that's a good thing.

You want the flexibility to be able to ebb and flow and adjust small parts of your formula to get to the desired outcome that works for you and the situation you are in. For the most optimal outcomes, you must be willing to assess each situation individually with the components of your core values: what the situation is, what outcome you're seeking, who's involved, what skills you have to address the situation, and what leadership style(s) you plan to embrace.

In addition to this framework, you also need a healthy infusion of finesse—the ability to utilize your own unique approach to a situation, which allows a dose of authenticity and deeper connection.

So, it's a perfect time to advance to another conversation: finessing your style.

8 Finessing Your Style

'll let the cat out of the bag right away so you don't get derailed by the word "finesse." Finessing your style is nothing more than being you. It's actually being *more* of you. In a world that is constantly directing us to be more of something else, instead of what and who we actually are, it's often hard to settle on what it means to actually embrace you and understand how you approach things. In this chapter, I'm encouraging you to do more of that throughout your leadership journey.

Let me share more about my journey in finessing my style.

For employees at an organization, getting performance reviews with some form of regularity is pretty typical. It's commonplace for your immediate leader to write and deliver your past year's performance results to you. In contrast, in the world of entrepreneurship (where I live), gathering feedback and insight about my work with an individual or an organization is critical, but it isn't going to happen unless I solicit it. In my pursuit of feedback, I gather it after almost every training or coaching engagement and I do this even if it is a client or organization that I've worked with time and time again. The feedback that I get pretty consistently is around my

style of delivery. There are four phrases that continually come up over
and over again:

- Engaging
- Relatable
- Inspires action
- Unique delivery

I have to take a moment and highlight one of the phrases: *unique
delivery*. While I am proud and grateful that clients consider my
leadership training engaging, relatable, and inspiring of action, I must
say that I am always proud to see *unique delivery*.

Here's why. Of the billions of people in the world, while you and
I likely have several things in common, none of us—no two
individuals (even those who are twins)—are exactly the same. And
that is amazing and special. For me, when I see that a client
recognizes this uniqueness that I willingly allow to shine through in
my presentations, it is a much larger compliment than they may
even realize.

There are hundreds of leadership consultancies across the world,
many of which teach the same concepts, same principles, and same
theories. But my clients choose to engage with me not only because
of the concepts, principles, and theories that I teach, but also
because of my unique delivery. And the only way I'm able to make
good on this is by embracing my own personal style of delivery—
finessing my style.

Leadership is an art and not a science. And it's a very good thing
that there is flexibility in how you approach leadership and how you
choose to handle situations where leadership skills are essential. The
reason why this is important is that people are nuanced. And because
we are, a certain level of flexibility and unique approaches are
required to make sure that you're connecting with people and the

organization and also getting necessary things done. The nuance of individuals is the perfect opportunity for you to use your finesse within the leadership world and uniquely connect based on your experiences, knowledge, or approach.

Let's take it one level further.

I want you to think of finesse very much as you would a fashion-related scenario. Wearing a black suit works in most professional situations—it's classic, it's clean, and it's uncontroversial. Your ability to incorporate a colored scarf, switch up your necktie, or add a pair of shoes with a pop of color are ways that you can take an outfit from drab to fab. It's also a way to let your personality shine through.

While there are basic core components of leadership, as we've explored throughout the book, remember that you are a unique part of the situation. Allowing your uniqueness and your personal finesse to shine through is what will elevate your leadership scenarios. Let's explore a few ways that you can finesse your style, make meaningful connections, and create impact not just for your benefit but also for the benefit of the others you're leading, directing, or even unknowingly influencing.

Identifying Your Style

This time, I'm not talking about your leadership style. It's about your overall style and approach. If I asked you about your general approach when addressing a difficult conversation, what would you say? That's what I mean when I ask what your style is. To further help you figure out what your *style* is, consider your answers to these questions:

- Do you like to address tough conversations head on and directly?
- Do you naturally utilize humor in your conversations?
- Do you prefer conversational pleasantries or would you rather get to the point?

When I think about my own personal style, it's a mix of tough love and humor. I can't profess to being the funniest person you'll meet, but I naturally gravitate toward infusing a bit of appropriate humor into my interactions.

Pinpointing Your Mannerisms

Most of us have repetitive mannerisms that can be pinpointed with a bit of intentional observing, documenting, and inquiring. Let's explore how you discover more about yourself by learning from you and learning from others.

The very first step in pinpointing your mannerisms is one that requires no physical actions at all, just your willingness. We have been who we are for quite some time and over time, we have settled more into who you are, what we are comfortable with, and what works for us (in some situations). The *some situations* part is one that I would like to highlight because, since situations vary, we have to be willing to handle them in different ways. If you attempt to tackle all situations the same way, you risk being inefficient, ineffective, and unsuccessful.

It would seem easy that we should be able to learn the most from the person who seemingly knows the most about us—ourselves, right? But it is often difficult to step outside of ourselves to conduct a neutral and unbiased assessment of who we are. While it can be challenging, it can be done and in two different ways:

1. Willingness to learn more about your style from you
2. Willingness to learn more about your style from others

Let's talk about you first.

Leadership Tip: There is only one you. The upside of this is that
you have certain unique qualities that may seem rare and even
evoke a sense of being different. On your leadership elevation
journey, it's essential that you embrace your uniqueness and the way
you finesse a situation, which may be different from the approaches
of others.

Learning from You

One of the best ways to learn from yourself is through documentation
and review. While being aware of what our style may be in real time,
by documenting our experiences and then reviewing it, we can
analyze ourselves while outside of the situation at hand. This can be
accomplished by journaling, either digitally or physically. Consistent
journaling allows us to observe trends and similarities in our
approach, instead of making snap judgments about how we may have
handled something in a one-off situation.

If you're trying to just get started with learning from yourself,
start doing it one day at a time. Begin by reflecting on the day and
your various situations. Ask yourself some of these questions:

- How did I initially address the day's challenges?

- What were my immediate reactions to situations? Did I panic
  first? Was I optimistic first? Did I lash out first?

- Do I tend to blame myself for any hiccups in the day? Do I tend
  to blame others?

Learning from Others

Just as you have the opportunity to learn from yourself, you have a
similar and sometimes more valuable opportunity to learn from

others. Because we often see ourselves much different from how we truly are, it's essential that we seek feedback from others. One of the best ways to do this is by commissioning your own 360 review.

If you're not already familiar, a 360 review is a performance tool that solicits feedback about someone from all directions: their managers, coworkers, direct reports, friends, and so on. While most people will only use this tool in a corporate setting, I'd like to challenge that approach. Because I'm asking you to embrace your ability to lead in environments outside of the workplace and because you are doing this every day even when you aren't trying to, it's helpful to know more about your style so that you can transparently assess if you need to adjust, modify, and elevate in some places.

You have the potential to be a leader in the workplace, in your home, among your friends, in your community, with your travel buddies—pretty much everywhere.

So soliciting feedback from worthy and valuable individuals who are truly capable and interested in providing it is to your benefit. The same questions that you asked yourself above can be the questions you ask of others to get more insight into your style and approach.

The Styles of Other Successful Leaders

It is recommended that you pay attention to the behaviors of leaders you admire. Sometimes you'll recognize that other leaders exhibit behaviors that you never realized were ones you should consider embracing for yourself. But even if you commit to embracing new leadership behaviors and skills, for them to be most effective, you need to embody them in a way that is authentic to you or else it won't translate well.

We all have a particular style that we gravitate toward. I challenge you to discover your style so that you can more intentionally and more thoughtfully connect with individuals on your leadership path.

Adjusting Your Style and Approach

While it is nice to know how you approach and address certain things, that's only the tip of the iceberg. The next questions that you should ask yourself after knowing how you are is:

Is this serving me? Could I get to where I want to be more effectively? Do I want to be perceived as someone who approaches things in that particular way?

The upside to learning about the way you approach things is that if required and desired, you can change. Just as we learned that there are many different leadership styles you can utilize to deal most effectively with a situation, there are options for you to adjust how you are approaching and reacting to things to get the optimal outcome for yourself and for your goals.

You should consider adjusting your style and approach if:

- You keep doing things the same way and you are not getting the outcomes you wanted.
- You get scathing or undesirable feedback from others that catches you off guard and is unexpected.
- You want to be seen and show up differently.

How to Adjust Your Style

Okay, take a deep breath and say to yourself, "I can do this."

While we've been busy being us for so long, we've also been busy getting comfortable with that. And, as we've learned throughout this book, we are often required to get comfortably uncomfortable when we want to get somewhere new or advance to our next level.

You can do hard and uncomfortable things.

Leadership Tip: Speaking of hard and uncomfortable things, it's the perfect time to mention that you've been doing hard and uncomfortable things for decades, yet somewhere in our lives we stop believing that we could or should do so. While you're exploring the concepts in this book that may not immediately make you feel comfortable, be the leader who reminds yourself, "I can do hard and uncomfortable things."

I know that the fast pace of the world makes us expect immediate action and swift results, but frequently we have to wait. There is often nothing wrong with waiting a bit. And speaking of waiting, I want to note that it's necessary for you to commit to a period of time of doing these things before you expect some real results and change. While it is often stated that it takes 21 days to form a habit, we all have different factors in our life where this amount of time may be too much or too little.

Thus, I'd like for you to set your own time frame of one week or more that you're going to commit to these steps and consistently follow them. If you'd like to adjust your style and approach, for at least one week straight and in every situation, commit to:

- Set your intentions mentally.
- Listen intently.
- Breathe.
- Try not to take things personally (unless they are personal).
- Watch your facial and body expressions. Are you communicating things that you really didn't intend to?
- Ask questions for clarity and understanding.
- Share what you know and what you don't know.
- Ensure there is shared understanding of what's next and what was discussed.

While we all end up being a certain *way* as part of our leadership journey, this *way* that we choose to conduct ourselves is based on the experiences, knowledge, and insight that we've collected through our life. And although this approach may have served us, we must ask ourselves: Is it still serving us? We have the ability to acquire new knowledge, adopt new behaviors, and make different choices.

We must be the kind of leader who is willing to modify our approach and our style to suit who we can and want to be. You can change your leadership style and approach. You've already started on the journey by picking up this book. Now let's keep going by understanding how to use our voice effectively.

9 Using Your Voice

Letting your voice be heard on your leadership journey is so important. Embracing the potential that you have something important to say, something essential to communicate and contribute, is a personal and essential part of this leadership journey.

Be mindful and embrace those words, particularly the word "potential." Embracing the fact that you have the potential to say something meaningful doesn't mean that you're talking just to talk. It means that if there is something essential that needs to be said, you will activate your courage and confidence and give yourself permission to speak up.

This chapter is dedicated to providing you with some tools and direction on how to get out of your head, and using your voice to say the words that bravely need to be said.

There are actually two parts to this journey of using your voice. Part one is the permission you have to give yourself that you have the right to speak. Part two consists of the tactical and actual words and phrases you speak after you give yourself permission to say something. Part one doesn't work without part two and part two doesn't work without part one. It's a package deal, and it's in your best interest to embrace both of these parts so that:

1. You know you have something to say.
2. You have the right words to say it.

Part 1: The Inner Work

Do any of these situations sound familiar to you?

- You're nervous that the question you want to ask is a stupid one.
- You wonder why you're in this meeting or in this setting in the first place.
- You realize you're the most junior person in the meeting.
- You think you don't have anything meaningful to contribute.
- You've never been a good or confident public speaker and you don't want to sound silly.
- You're not sure if what you want to say has already been covered.

Let me first take a moment to validate any of the feelings that come along with these statements. And let me also say that I have personally felt impacted by many of the statements above.

While I have had the distinct pleasure and privilege of being on stage with large audiences since the fourth grade, and although I am very used to using my voice on large and small stages across the globe, I still have doubts about my value or what I'm about to contribute—often.

But my job and commitment to myself is that I don't allow those quick thoughts in my mind to completely eradicate and destroy the impact opportunity and value that I contribute toward a situation.

My hope for you is that you embrace that same thought process.

My goal here is to provide you with tools and resources so that when that doubt creeps in and when you feel overwhelmed and in a place where you begin to think you shouldn't use your voice, you shouldn't speak up or say what needs to be said that no one else is saying, you can utilize the skills provided in this chapter.

It's also best for you to embrace an "out-of-body experience" as you formulate your thoughts around the value that you contribute to a certain situation by using your voice. Instead of asking yourself, "Why am I here?" or "What value do I bring?" ask:

1. Why did X invite me here?
2. What value does X believe I bring to this situation?

The goal is to get to a place where the value and the impact that you're going to contribute to a situation is understood and you recognize why you're supposed to be somewhere and why you must speak up. Always remember this is a journey. If you initially need to learn more about your value through the eyes of someone else first, then that's going to be what you must first embrace to keep going on your journey.

The thing about giving yourself permission to use your voice is that it also serves you personally as well. Remember that leadership isn't this thing that just coalesces in the workplace, so think about the moments when you're dining and traveling and shopping and parenting and dating and attending happy hours. Those moments also present opportunities for you to use your voice and be the leader you know you are deep within. I dig deeper into these opportunities in Chapter 10 but for now, more inner work.

Manage Your Self-Talk and Self-Doubt

It would be a huge missed opportunity if we didn't address the very real and very challenging part of using your voice that has nothing to do with outside forces, outside factors, or anyone or anything else but you. Have you ever experienced a moment of recognizing that there's a little voice in the back of your head that is talking you out of the thing that you're trying to do—including maybe even using your voice?

I understand the uncomfortable feeling that sometimes comes along with simply just speaking up, not because I'm not prepared, not because I didn't practice and not because I didn't know what I was talking about, but simply because of this little unidentified faceless voice that pops up at the most inopportune and unexpected time and makes me question everything.

I've been in many rooms throughout my career where I knew that I had something to say and I knew that I wanted to raise my hand and give input or feedback or insight. But that inner anxiety and daunting self-doubt had me silently questioning if I had something of value to contribute and forced me to keep my words muffled or unsaid. That feeling was further exacerbated when I was formally diagnosed with anxiety disorder at the age of 19. So there's a need for constant management of feeling overwhelmed when it comes to speaking and presenting.

I've learned how to manage being consumed by the overwhelming feelings of self-doubt, negative self-talk, and even anxiety to muster up the confidence to say what needs to be said. After over 30 years of experience on stage and impacting over 25,000 people across the globe in leadership-centric areas, I learned several things prove to be true:

1. When you begin believing that your voice has value and that you have meaningful things to say, expressing the words gets easier. Using your voice becomes more comfortable the more you do it.

2. Whether you feel a question is silly or not, ask it. A question is a question and questions need answering.

3. Practice makes us better, and we're all capable of getting better.

4. Focus on listening first, then use your words as a tool to address what you learned from listening. It will save you time and energy and build stronger relationships.

Now that we've explored how to manage your own inner voice and inner feelings, let's dive into the world of listening.

Listening as a Tool to Use Your Voice Better

One of the most important tools you have in your tool kit as you're giving yourself permission to use your voice more has nothing at all to do with your voice. It's a simple six-letter word that is used, misused, abused, and neglected. This little word is the source of misunderstanding, arguments, and relationship ruiners. That word is "listen."

Our ability—or inability—to *listen*, intentionally and fully, is critical. I have three key tips on being a better listener:

- **Listen to listen.** The outcome of your listening doesn't necessarily mean that you have to give a long, drawn-out response. Sometimes it's necessary to just listen and acknowledge that something was said.

- **Listen to understand.** While the world riddles us with so many things to pay attention to and focus on simultaneously, it's our job—in the moment—to understand what's being presented to us versus rushing to the next seemingly important thing that's in front of us.

- **Listen, not to fix.** This is the absolute hardest thing for me to do while listening. I am a certified fixer! When someone presents a challenge, even if it's not directed at me, I immediately go into a mental fix-it-now mind frame. I start thinking about how I can support this person and help them fix whatever it is they are communicating to me. *This is a mistake.* This turns me from active listener to partial listener and partial fixer in real time. This is bad because 1) I'm not listening anymore, and 2) it may be a situation that actually doesn't need to be fixed at all.

If these listening tips are embraced, it becomes easier to use your voice. Think about it. If you have diligently listened to someone's words and you've understood them, any words that come out of your mouth must be in alignment with what they just said because you fully listened.

Let me share my truth with you.

My name is Jacqueline M. Baker and I have a short attention span. I am fully aware that I always have to work a bit harder to avoid getting distracted or thrown off track in a conversation. Sometimes what happens is that, although I am fully in listening mode, my mind starts to wander a little bit. While I try to ensure that when I'm with someone I am giving them the attention and respect their voice deserves, unfortunately my mind suddenly starts to wander when instead I need to respectfully continue to engage with this person.

When this happens, in comes a tactic that I keep in my back pocket just in case my sneaky little attention span has tricked me yet again. It's a simple phrase that allows me to voice what I heard, but also leave room for what I didn't. That phrase is: "What I think I heard you say was _____." This allows me to voice the other person's words and also get clarity on what I perhaps did not hear. This tool is not designed for or encouraging you to half listen to people and then throw out the "what I think I heard you say" phrase every single time. It's designed to be a tool in your leadership tool kit so that you can listen appropriately, recenter yourself in the moment, and also use your voice appropriately as well.

Listening to other people in a real-time moment isn't a passive activity. When you accept it as such, it positions you to be involved in it intentionally, instead of treating it like background noise.

I want you to recognize listening as a benefit for both you as the listener and the other person as the speaker. When used effectively, it lets the other person say what is needed and it lets you get the details you need to make an informed and intentional response.

Listen more effectively so you can respond more intentionally.

Believe That Your Words Have Meaning

Just because you aren't always the go-to person on a subject matter or concern doesn't mean that there isn't something that you have the potential to contribute to it. Your ability to use your voice has nothing to do with someone else's inability to ask you. Sometimes it's a matter of recognizing that you have unique insight and a unique perspective based on what you know and what your experiences are.

Think of an experience where a topic was being discussed and you were playing mental double Dutch, asking yourself, "Should I say something or shouldn't I?" Then, almost at the moment of you saying something, when the person speaking gives the absolutely final concluding opportunity for someone to ask a question, another person jumps in and you realize that what this other person is commenting on is exactly what you were going to ask. So then you spend the next few minutes mentally beating yourself up for not speaking up and then you partially miss the answer to the question the other person asked.

Yes, I've seen this story countless times and been the main character in it as well.

By default, your words already have meaning. But you can easily reduce the worth of the meaning if you don't use the words. Using your words comfortably is like working your muscles—the more you do it, the better you get at it and the better you become. You begin to be less apprehensive about using them. But this entire process starts with you doing one thing: believing that your words have value and meaning and then using them.

Since we've spent some time on the inner work, let's redirect our attention to the outer work—the actual words we use to support the decision that we made internally.

Part 2: The Outer Work

Our roles as leaders aren't just to lead ourselves but to also lead others. While the process of leading will never be perfect, we should be committed to approaching it with a spirit of advancement and elevation, as opposed to minimization and doubt. One of the best ways to avoid this minimization and doubt and to lead others is through intentional word choice. As you begin to be more confident in using your voice, you will start to elevate in your speaking style and word choice. But in the beginning you may feel like you're stumbling over your words and need to rely more on some of your staple filler words and phrases (um, like, so, etc.).

Use Filler Words

While I do not encourage you to overuse filler words or even use them intentionally, embracing filler words as you work to find other ways and utilize other strategies to get your point across may be necessary at first. But as you practice and become savvier at using your voice intentionally, filler words will begin to fall off. Just like any other thing that we do, this will evolve so that you learn to utilize more effective tools.

- Before the dry cleaners were available, we handwashed everything.
- Before the invention of the electric can opener, we had a manual option.

- Before automatic windows in our vehicles, we rolled them down with a hand crank.
- Before Bluetooth and digital music, we played 8-tracks, cassettes, and CDs.
- Before remote controls, we physically got up (or sent our children) to change the TV channel.

I'm not asking you to embrace filler words all the time or actively make them a part of your vocabulary. Instead, don't be so hard on yourself if you have to use them when you are working on using your voice.

I want you to think of filler words and phrases as akin to a journey a child goes on when learning how to walk. The child's goal is to walk, but they don't just wake up one day and start walking. There is some stumbling involved; sometimes they're going to plop down on their bottom and even occasionally take a massive tumble. But eventually most kids go on to become refined walkers and maybe even runners at some point.

As we find better solutions and become comfortable with them, the previous options become obsolete. But let's face it, many of the original options are still options, right? We can still handwash clothing and crank open cans and manually change television channels, and I'll also take this moment to confess that I still have a number of CDs and DVDs that I break out every now and then.

So while you will upgrade your vocabulary and the way in which you formulate words and phrases and voice them, filler words will still be within your reach when absolutely necessary.

Avoid Certain Phrases

To ensure that you're not minimizing your words or feeling that they need to be qualified, it's important to recognize a few phrases that decrease your message value. Try to avoid these self-deprecating phrases:

- **"I believe this was already said," or "To piggyback off what they just said."** Remember that you're speaking with intent and to add value to a conversation or scenario. If a subject has already been covered and addressed thoroughly, it is permissible to express that you agree and to endorse the statement, but to restart a conversation about it all over again isn't adding meaningful value.

- **"I'm not sure if anyone cares about this."** This devalues your statement before it even fully comes out of your mouth. If you've listened appropriately to preceding conversations (if there were any) and you feel you have something meaningful to say, say it, but without a caveat that plants an unnecessary negative seed in people's minds.

- **"Not to be all negative but . . ."** Most people don't want negative energy injected into a situation. If you know that a potential statement will change the tone and energy of the room, there's a way to preface it that doesn't need to be laced with negativity or even a mere mention of the word.

- **"This might be silly, but . . ."** This phrase comes in many different forms. It can also disguise itself as "This is a dumb question, but . . ." or "Perhaps this isn't a good idea, but . . ." or "This might not work, but . . ." Whatever flavor this phrase comes in, don't use it and don't share it. The words that you choose to come out of your mouth have meaning and are intentional. There's no time, no space, and no value to you supplanting the ideas that your words are silly, dumb, aren't a good idea, or may not work.

Diversify Your Word Choice

Now, I can't just throw out a lot of things not to say without addressing what the appropriate options might be. Remember that we're not on a path of perfection where we're trying to say all the things right every time, but we are on a path of committing to put our best foot forward with intention so that our words land in the ears of those listening in a way that is digestible, actionable, and meaningful. Even if you're presenting a topic or asking a question and you're unsure about asking it, here are some more positively positioned statements that will allow your words to land more effectively:

- "I'd like to offer another perspective."
- "Let me make sure that I'm understanding this approach."
- "I'd like to offer an alternative option that might not have been considered."

The second edition of the 20-volume *Oxford English Dictionary* contains 171,476 words. There is always an alternative way to make a statement that evokes a different response and elicits a different emotion. While we can easily gravitate toward the words and phrases that we always hear being used, we're not in pursuit of easy or simple. We're in pursuit of effective and intentional words. The next time you're in a situation where you're gearing up to use your voice, ask yourself, "Are the words that are about to come out of my mouth being said with intent and in the spirit of advancement and elevation and not diminishing"?

Taking just a moment to quickly consider this and also committing it to practice will allow you to make easier and quicker decisions about what to say and how to say it.

As you've noticed, I have refrained from using the words "public speaking" in this chapter. It's not that I don't want to encourage you to speak publicly on your leadership journey, but while you will need to use your voice to engage in public speaking activities, you don't have to grace stages or be deeply immersed in speaking engagements to give yourself permission to use your voice. You've been using your voice for decades, having personal and business conversations about all different kinds of things. This chapter and the simple act of using your voice isn't about speaking in front of stadiums of folks. It's about the everyday impact you can make in your corner of the world by being intentional with your choice of words to use and not use.

Leadership Tip: As someone who has been on massive stages for close to 30 years, I would be remiss if I told you that the nervousness that comes along with speaking publicly goes away completely. And I'm not talking about just speaking on large stages, I'm talking about all stages, from 25 audience members to 25,000. What does change is how you manage the nervousness: 25 years ago, it might have taken me 25 minutes of speaking in front of a crowd before those jitters subsided. Now, those same jitters have come and gone by the time I hit the 20-second mark because I've learned how to manage them. Be the leader that gives yourself permission to use your voice so that you can build up the correct muscle and tools to practice, improve, and impact other leaders around you with your intentional words.

Now, you might decide that you want to grace stages and change lives with your voice—and you can. With these simple tips, you're on your way. But if you decide to be an everyday leader of yourself and never climb the stairs to give a keynote or presentation, you'll be prepared to do that as well.

In whatever situation you find yourself, always remember how to use your voice effectively:

- Be mindful of filler words and give yourself permission to graduate from training wheels to a full-fledged bike.
- Accept that using your voice is a learning journey.
- Continually reassure yourself of the value that your words have the opportunity to contribute.
- Speak with intention.
- Know when it's time to use your voice with high-quality input and when it's time to let someone else use theirs.

Using your voice and the value of your words is an important part of your leadership journey. That journey extends beyond your professional aspirations. There are many ways to lead every day, in all aspects of our lives, and using your voice allows you to do that more effectively.

Your journey to become a more eloquent communicator and speaker might initially be riddled with a few bumps, bruises, and filler words. But your continued commitment to giving yourself permission to use your voice, practice, and speak with intention is how you elevate from amateur to confident communicator.

10 Everyday Ways to Lead

'm not exactly saying that this is my favorite chapter, but I do have a lot of love and respect for this chapter. This is my opportunity to help you see that leadership and its benefits surround us every day and have the potential to be embedded in everything we do.

I do recognize that the word "leadership" closely resonates with people in a professional or business setting. If you asked someone where you would most likely see leaders leading and you gave them three options:

- In the workplace
- On the golf course
- At a restaurant

people are most likely going to pick "in the workplace." But I'm going to push back and challenge that. Solid leadership is the amalgamation of several core areas:

- Self-awareness
- Personality traits

- Communication
- Agility and adaptability
- Delegation
- Innovation and change maker

And, since we're engaging in activities outside the workplace every day that allow us to strengthen skills in these six areas, leadership can be cultivated, grown, and refined outside of the workplace.

But for this to work, I have to ask you to do something (again). I want you to embrace your leadership role all day every day, rather than waiting until you walk into one particular place to put on your leadership cape. Recognize that whether you're at the gym, in the office, at happy hour, on vacation, or running a meeting, you are a leader.

I'm not someone who is serious and in business mode every single day of my life and in every single situation. I don't encourage you to be that way either. I don't expect that you spend every moment of your life with a serious scowl, walking around with your leadership ruler and citation pad trying to force people into being super serious about leadership. That's not an effective way to approach any of this.

What I do want to encourage you to do is to embrace your inner leader and know that there are spaces and places for you to lead independent of where you might be at any given moment. And by embracing your inner leader 365 days a year, 24 hours a day, 7 days a week, it's easier for you to elevate. It's easier for you to acquire new skills and it's easier for you to get to your next level because you're always being a leader.

But what does that *really* mean? It's story time.

After an eight-year foray as co-founder of an event management company in the early 2000s, I looked around my hometown of

Detroit and noticed that the area had a need. While there were some organizations teaching etiquette to young leaders, I found that it wasn't conducted in a developmental way that translated to long-term professional opportunities. In the spirit of being the change I wanted to see, I launched a company called Scarlet Communications, with a clear goal of helping people become more confident through utilizing etiquette skills. From dining to communication to travel to golf to social media, we began impacting youth and adult students across the country.

Considering that the company at the time was solely focused on modern etiquette and I was the primary instructor, this etiquette knowledge I taught spilled over into my personal world. Although we covered a wealth of topics outside of dining etiquette, I recognize that most people's minds venture toward dining when they think of the word "etiquette." So let's use that as an example.

Do I know how to instruct my students on the proper way to utilize a wine glass, navigate a dining table, and tip appropriately, and which utensils are used for which courses? *Of course I do.*

When I go out to eat, will you see me actively utilizing these dining standards? *Yes you will.*

I'm not using these standards as a result of not being willing to turn off business. It's because I'm a leader in this space, not just between the hours of 8 and 4, but all day every day. If I turn off this practice of navigating the table the right way when I'm off work, the next day when I have to go back into "business" mode, I have to mentally adjust back into it, instead of just always mentally being there.

I don't want you to feel like you constantly must be on and in business mode all of the time, because I am most certainly not. Instead, I want you to think about the many spaces and activities that you have the opportunity to engage in completely outside of the workplace and where you knowingly or unknowingly are leading and are probably doing a really good job at it.

While there are varying degrees of what these things are, depending on who you are, some common scenarios are:

- Going on vacation
- Accepting a date
- Everyday transit to and from home
- Eating at a restaurant
- Taking your children on a playdate
- Working out at the gym
- Visiting your religious institution
- Attending your neighborhood HOA meeting
- Standing in a friend's wedding
- Going grocery shopping
- Playing golf with friends

Leadership Tip: Your skeptical mind may make you want to question if there are opportunities to really discover and elevate your leadership abilities in all scenarios. I suggest you take the opportunity to try a different approach. Instead of approaching your growth opportunity from a space of skepticism and doubt, be the leader who commits to discovery rather than suspicion. The best way to redirect your mind to a place of positivity and enlightenment is by using the words "How might I?" *How might I utilize my time and experiences while I'm at the next golf outing to build stronger relationships and communicate more clearly about what I want?*

To give you some insight and direction on how you might explore ways to embrace leadership outside the workplace but still live a fun, interesting, unstuffy, and "regular" life, let's map some of the core leadership areas outside of business situations. Those areas include self-awareness, communication, agility and adaptability, and delegation.

Self-Awareness

As you just learned, in one of the lanes of my life I teach modern etiquette internationally. Etiquette is not a very common career choice and I very rarely randomly encounter other people who do this work, but people generally know exactly what etiquette is. While most people closely relate etiquette to dining, in fact the different etiquette topics I explore and teach are vast, including golf etiquette, social media etiquette, travel etiquette, communication etiquette, and grooming etiquette. Teaching all these topics allows me to do one essential thing: help people start the things that they want to do and advance to their next level of leadership

For the moment, though, and in service of bringing this point home, let's stay with the topic of dining etiquette. Imagine that I'm out with a newer set of friends having casual conversation over a meal. All sorts of discussions are happening and none happen to be about our careers. While I am perfectly fine discussing the fact that I'm a modern etiquette expert when the time is right, in dining settings (especially when I'm with a newer group of friends) I'm not looking to shout from the rooftops that this is an area I operate in. I'm proud of my work in this space and continue to serve clients all across the world, but I know that in dining settings people get uncomfortable or self-conscious when they find out that an etiquette expert is sitting next to them. This doesn't mean I won't talk about this career lane of mine at all. I'm just mindful about being overly vocal about it as a focal part of a conversation over a meal if I'm not there to teach or counsel on that particular subject.

Self-awareness is a muscle that must be worked on in order to be improved. Although it seems that we should be the experts on ourselves, sometimes we need a little intentional work to realize more about ourselves to be more effective communicators, listeners, and leaders. If you're looking to be more self-aware, try:

- Taking personality assessments
- Getting regular feedback
- Keeping a journal and regularly documenting your experiences (and reflect on them)

As much as we may want to believe we are a certain way, only through self-reflection and feedback do we really learn our level of self-awareness, and then we should be willing to make decisions on how we utilize this information to be a more self-aware and elevated leader.

Personality Traits

There are things that are just uniquely you. We previously explored the fact that billions of people walk the earth every day, yet somehow there is still only one you. While you may share similar personality traits with other people, our various leadership opportunities and growth can benefit from both our personality traits and the uniqueness of each of us. You can continue to discover more about your personality traits through the various personality assessments like DiSC, Myers-Briggs, and others.

You may in fact be the one person in your family or friend group who sees things differently, takes a different approach, or is willing to go against the grain because of your personality makeup. While this (sometimes) defiant approach of yours may feel fleeting, controversial, or even counterproductive, it's still necessary for someone to be willing to raise their hand to question the unquestionable, propose a different approach, or even start something over from scratch. Our natural or adopted personality traits can be the permission that we need to discover a new approach or solution that no one else is willing to see at the most opportune times.

Communication

Imagine that your friend of 15 years got engaged recently and she has asked you to stand in her wedding. While you're honored to be considered, you're signed up to stand in three other weddings around the same time as hers. As much as you want to be a great friend, you know that the right thing to do is to clearly communicate to your friend:

- You're honored to be considered.
- You want to make sure that any commitment you make for such an important day, you can fully show up for.
- You're already overcommitted.
- You don't want this decision to impact the quality of your friendship.

Although your friend might be taken aback at first that you aren't able to fully commit, you've done the right thing by being a leader who communicates clearly and directly about your inability to commit to her wedding activities. In just about every situation, it's important to communicate to the other parties involved so they have the most current and up-to-date details. Don't leave people hanging. Don't commit to something you don't have time for—or indicate that you do have time but don't fully engage in the end. Make it clear what others can expect of you.

Communication is one of those magical skills that cut across every sector of our lives. It's also one of those deeply multifaceted skills that seems simple in nature but below the surface is deeply complicated. This is because communication reaches far beyond the words you say.

While all the words above could be stated to your friend and in the same order as listed, the way in which you say them, the tone you project, the distance between you two as you speak, and even your hand gestures all play a part in how the message is delivered and received. Beyond the words that you use, there are six other areas that you should keep in mind as you're looking to communicate intentionally and effectively:

- Facial expressions
- Body movement and posture
- Gestures
- Touch
- Space
- Eye contact

Only 7% of communication happens through our words. The other whopping 93% occurs through our nonverbals, like facial expressions, body movements, and so forth. So remember to align your words with your nonverbals for an overall effective communication approach.

Agility and Adaptability

Imagine that you were asked out on a date a couple of weeks ago and you gladly accepted. You've noticed that over the past few weeks your date has been getting clarity about the things you like, what you enjoy doing, and what your preferences are. Then, when the day arrived, the grand plans your date made fell through because the location had a massive flood. Your date proposed an alternative plan of a stroll through the park and a picnic. Although you were disappointed, you decided to embrace agility, adaptability, and flexibility instead of expressing disappointment for what could have been.

As much as we want things to come together seamlessly and for things to go 100% as planned, rarely does that occur. Our ability to embrace the unknown and "go with the flow" positions us to see the positives and the pleasant surprises in unexpected situations. This commitment to embracing agility and adaptability in individual situations is important, but it is also essential when you're setting expectations for yourself. Consider what you may have thought about what you were (or were not) a couple of years ago from a leadership standpoint before you picked up this book.

Your ability to be flexible even with the thoughts about yourself, your potential, and your opportunities is of immense value. Be willing to embrace things that are unexpected and not clearly within your view.

Delegation

The annual BBQ that you've been hosting for five years is around the corner. Unlike other years, this year has been an incredibly overwhelming one with two deaths in your family, a personal health scare, and a recent unexpected job adjustment where you have had to take on more responsibilities. While you are committed to seeing this sixth annual BBQ through, you're stressing about how you'll get it all done this time. Several of your friends know about what's going on in your life and have offered to help. Although you normally execute this entire BBQ yourself, deep inside you know that you need some help. You finally decide to delegate some tasks so that the event can happen and you won't be overwhelmed by it all.

The magic of delegation is that the thing you were ultimately after to get done can still be done, but with a bit of assistance.

Furthermore, there is an opportunity for you to actually enjoy the outcome more because, through delegation, you can:

- Share the breadth of the work with others.

- Inspire and support other people to elevate in their leadership journey by offering them visibility and skill elevation opportunities.

- Actually enjoy the outcomes and not be burned out by trying to do it all.

There are a million ways to get the exact same tasks completed. By embracing delegation, you're allowing the discovery of other ways to elevate as a leader while also supporting the elevation of others at the same time.

Innovation and Change Maker

Several paces down the road in Chapter 14, I dive into the world of innovation and highlight some companies that didn't embrace their innovation opportunities, which led to the demise of several organizations. Well, unfortunately, guess who else can be impacted by not embracing innovation?

That's right: you!

Innovation isn't a word that you need to shy away from or leave only to the creative and technical people in your life. Instead, embrace your innovation and change maker spirit to simply identify ways to do something better, more effectively, and even more efficiently.

Imagine that you've been hosting a game night at your house quarterly for friends for years. Although you love to do it, you spend the following 48 hours afterwards putting your home back together. Once the pandemic reared its head in early 2020, you found yourself with no opportunity to host this thing that brings you so much joy.

Although you initially could not fathom fitting your game night into a virtual format, you give it a try to **test and learn**. To your surprise, this innovative approach works because:

- Your guests don't have to drive 90 minutes to get to your lovely yet rurally located home.

- You save a massive amount of money by not being committed to purchasing hundreds of dollars in food and beverages.

- You learn a new technology that you can utilize in other parts of your life.

- You evade the commitment of having to clean up your home to get it back to where it was pre-game night.

While this particular example could be applicable for lots of different types of events, it's ultimately meant to get your wheels turning. I recognize that the words "innovation" and "change maker" are often associated with big, sweeping initiatives that change the way that our worlds work and how we operate. But accept that you are not forbidden from personally embracing those words. You too can be an innovator and a change maker who tries new things, takes different approaches, and incorporates new approaches that impact your world, both personally and professionally. Commit to giving yourself permission to try new things and utilize innovative approaches that improve your life, expand your experiences, and elevate your leadership opportunities.

The opportunities to flex our leadership muscles outside of the workplace are all around us. I would actually argue that there are more opportunities to lead freely outside of the workplace than there are in the workplace, since in so many of our jobs, we're expected to "stay in our lane."

As you continue to give yourself permission to lead and elevate in your journey, keep your eyes open for opportunities to refine your skills in both business and nonbusiness settings. Your opportunities to be an effective leader can permeate in all areas of your life.

If you're struggling to find where else you might be able to stretch and develop your leadership muscles, Chapter 11 is calling your name.

11 Finding New Opportunities

Early one Sunday morning, as I was deep into the groove of writing this book, a dear friend of mine sent me a text message. While he and I have been good friends since we both worked at the Royal Oak YMCA in metro Detroit more than 15 years ago, we're the kind of friends who probably only communicate with each other a few times a year. Yet every time we do connect, it's meaningful, it's memorable, and it's genuine.

So this time when he reached out to me, his message started like it always does, "How's it going Jax?" Although I was in the throes of writing, I quickly broke my deep concentration to respond to him because I know these messages are few and far between. He shared with me that he recalled I was on a corporate board and that he had recently been asked to be a chair of the board for an organization that he was involved with. He also shared that he was incredibly fearful and anxious about assuming this position. He never had aspirations of being the board chair and was quite surprised when someone asked him. Now, of course, because of who I am, I quickly assured him that he was capable and ready, so that any doubt that he had in his mind would be minimized.

I tell you this story to illustrate that many times opportunities are presented to us and if we're not willing to be brave and bold and to open our eyes to these occasions, we can quickly disregard them or even respond immediately, "I'm not ready."

We can fall into the trap of disregarding and forgetting the skill set and qualifications that we have that uniquely position us to be ready to lead. For example, my friend has a doctorate, and he is one of the most compassionate and empathetic people I know. He has a wealth of experience in the audio education field and is highly regarded among his peers. So my response wouldn't be "Why would someone think of him for this position?" but excitement that my friend will put his collective skills together to serve in a higher leadership capacity.

Also, one of the reasons I was deeply excited and passionate about advising my friend is because his situation is very similar from mine. I serve on a corporate board for a global packaging and recycling organization. It was the first corporate board I ever served on. At the time I began, I was in my 30s, I was the only woman, and I was the only person of color on the board. And although I've shared accolades and accomplishments and things that I have refined in service of the work that I do, it was certainly a different feeling and a different experience of embracing the idea of being on this corporate board with professionals, many of whom are 20 to 30 years my senior. While of course this experience came with some level of doubt, now several years into serving in this capacity, I've learned a lot about how to approach these commitments and how to be successful at them.

While these opportunities were presented to my friend and me in an unexpected way, that won't always be the case for everyone. Some opportunities will be magically presented to us, but other times we will have to search for them and be intentional about what we want.

Let's explore these two potential opportunity paths:

Path 1: Pay attention to your everyday interactions and your everyday experiences, and embrace ways to lead that are literally served up and presented to you.

Path 2: Create opportunities for yourself. This path is likely also around you each and every day as well, but sometimes it requires a little bit more work and a lot more intention and purposefulness.

You should start this section by being in great spirits. You've already taken the most important step in being ready to receive leadership opportunities and that is embracing the fact that you are a leader. By embracing new opportunities, you are recommitting to your leadership journey.

The mantra is this: *"Today and every day I am a leader and I'm ready to take the journey to define and refine my leader within!"*

Now, let's explore how you can make yourself available to the leadership opportunities around you.

Let It Be Known

I have some close friends who are looking forward to having a mate, entertaining the possibility of marriage and even children. When we dig a little deeper and discuss how that might happen for them, they're unsure, which is understandable. At the same time my follow-up question is always this: "Are you in the right spaces and right conversations for that to even be a possibility?"

Now I know the dating scene is tricky, but the reality is that if you want to date someone or have a relationship with someone, it's not super likely that this person is just going to magically come knocking at your door without you putting in any kind of work.

Embrace this concept as it relates to identifying leadership opportunities. It has to be known. People have to know that it is something you're open to, something you're interested in, and something you're ready to move forward on. Let's discuss some ways that you can let it be known that you want to receive new leadership opportunities and elevate.

In the Workplace

Tell your immediate leader. When we work with people day in and day out, we often assume at some point that they know exactly what we're thinking and exactly what we're interested in. Do you feel like it's just a given and this person should assume this? Does your immediate leader (whomever you report to directly) know that you are interested in leadership development opportunities? While I hope that whoever your leader is embraces their role in managing and leading you, this might not be the case. You may have to compensate for the fact that they're still growing in their leadership journey as well. Let your immediate leader know that you're interested in refining specific skills and open to opportunities to do so. This might mean you take the lead on a new project, becoming the point person for a new program, or even acting as backup to someone who is serving point on a project or initiative. The goal here is to make it clear that you want to elevate and that there are specific skills you want to refine as you elevate.

Make it known among your peers. Typically, when we want to achieve something or elevate, we need to network upwards. Think about the number of people in your realm who are reachable to you immediately. How are you utilizing or leveraging those individuals? Think about someone in your workplace who might be working on a huge project and might need a little bit of help. They may never think to connect with you and ask you for this assistance, perhaps assuming that it's inappropriate or that you're unavailable. Take the road less traveled and embrace the wealth of opportunities that may be sitting just on the other side of you, on the other side of that cubicle, on the other side of that wall, or maybe even completely across the organization.

Get outside of your daily realm of operation. Consider this familiar chain of events: Wake up, hit snooze, snooze again, get out of bed, use the restroom, brush teeth, shower, put on clothes, rush to get coffee, grab a bite of food, hop in transportation, get to work, put on a smile, get in the elevator, get to desk, turn on computer, check emails, have meetings, eat lunch, have an afternoon snack, close down computer, get in transportation, get home.

It is so easy for us to repeat our cycles and our daily routines over and over and over again with no modifications. It's also easy for us to stay in our own little sections of our workplace without taking interest in or taking advantage of the opportunities that present themselves. Your workplace might have a number of different opportunities for you to lead that you were ignoring because they're not a part of your everyday routine. Consider these options:

- **Join a corporate affinity group.** Many corporate organizations have groups designated for women, for people of color, for Latinx, for LGBTQ individuals, for parents, and others. Although you may have not joined one previously and although you ignore the membership drive emails every time they hit your inbox, it might be time to take a second look. Many companies have opportunities for you to lead initiatives, lead conversations, and lead change.

- **Lead a cross-enterprise project.** Sometimes there are opportunities for you to participate across your organization that may impact or benefit the department you serve in. Keep an eye out for these and take the opportunity when it arises.

Outside the Workplace

Before we advance into taking advantage of opportunities to lead outside of the workplace, let me acknowledge a fundamental truth and potential reality for you.

Letting it be known in your friend and social circles that you want to elevate in your leadership journey has the potential to feel super awkward. It may feel weird because normally, you're not thinking of elevating your leadership skills in nonformal business environments. Still, you're doing things that designate you as a leader in both business and social settings, so acknowledge that and use it.

Choose your accountability group wisely. It is unnecessary to shout out to the rooftops to each and every friend or associate that you're looking for ways to elevate in your leadership journey. I mean, if we're just being honest here, everyone doesn't care. This journey you're on isn't being done for recognition or for praise, but for elevation in pursuit of your goals. While you may tell a friend, discreetly, don't feel the need to let everyone in on your approach.

You can simply identify a friend or two and say this: *"I'm working on some large goals and in pursuit of that, I'm being mindful to modify a few behaviors and I'm hoping you can tactfully hold me accountable for that."*

Make It Less About You

Although this book is about you and your leadership journey, the process of elevating doesn't need to be all about you. Many times we are able to get where we need to be without being out front, in the spotlight, or the main attraction. So let's explore how you can elevate by making things less about you.

In the Workplace

Most workplaces have a zillion different things going on at the same time. Some of them you're aware of and some things you're completely clueless about. The upside to the fact that there are lots of things going on that you aren't necessarily plugged into is that they pose an opportunity for you to learn and for you to assist. While of course many of us have commitments and day-to-day responsibilities that are directly tied to our work, this is a unique opportunity for you to accomplish several things:

- Let people know that you're interested in learning more and developing more leadership skills.

- Take your head out of just your lane and into a level of awareness of what's going on around you.

- Embrace that by being willing to be aware and learn about other things, you are ultimately strengthening the skills that you are currently acting on in your day-to-day work.

While the first step of this opportunity realm could be letting it be known by telling people you're available and want to develop as a leader in a particular space, you could also have a more specific goal of trying to help others. Imagine that there's someone on your team who is tasked with a rather large project that involves an extensive amount of work on a platform you're pretty familiar with. Offer up an hour or two of your time over a two-week period to assist them with this project. They're getting something out of it in the form of an extra set of hands, and you're getting a sense of how you operate when you're not leading something. You're learning how to give input and insight in a short period of time. Perhaps most importantly, you're learning about this new project that you previously didn't have any insight into.

While I recognize what I'm asking you to do is add some additional work to your day, consider it part of taking ownership over your leadership journey. We all have 168 hours in a week, but how we choose to utilize and manage those hours should be more up to us rather than left in the hands of others. By taking this approach, you own your path rather than just letting your path be served up to you.

Outside the Workplace

Think about the last time that you volunteered somewhere, selflessly gave your time or even donated some funds. Remind yourself of how good and fulfilling that felt, even in some cases unexpectedly awesome. As you're pursuing opportunities for yourself, I know that it feels like the first thing we should do is put ourselves first, and there are moments in your life when you should absolutely do that. But also remember that putting others first can serve them and also serve you as well. If you're trying to work on your team-building skills, maybe there's a unique opportunity for you to volunteer at a local community center, soup kitchen, or youth organization. There are likely other individuals there who are looking to do the same work that you're doing and guess what—there's going to be a need to work together as a team. And, while your primary goal as a volunteer for any organization that does this kind of work is going to be serving their mission, at the same time you're able to work on development and leadership skills. Think about it. What are the opportunities around you that will allow you to serve others while also truly serving yourself?

Get Uncomfortable

Being comfortable feels good and safe and fulfilling. Yet being comfortable all the time keeps us in the same place. On your journey of elevating in your leadership and discovering the leader within you, it will require you to step into new spaces that can often be unknown, uncharted, and uncomfortable. I challenge you to give yourself permission to be comfortably uncomfortable. When you initiate the discomfort, it puts you in charge and lets you take ownership over the discomfort. I do recognize that discomfort feels, well, uncomfortable. But our newest opportunities are often on the other side of a little discomfort.

In the Workplace

A few years ago when I was serving as vice president of startup programming at one of the nation's largest nonprofits, I was asked to speak on a panel about the intersection of health tech and fin tech. I was often tapped to be a part of these conversations because of the types of startup that I was consistently tasked with identifying and learning about. As a result, speaking about this particular subject didn't give me a lot of pause. I showed up at this conference not really thinking super hard about the topic or the conversation, because I had spoken about this topic many times previously.

Well, to my surprise when I stepped foot inside the JW Marriott in downtown Washington, DC, I couldn't help noticing that not only was my panel about health tech and fin tech but there was also a significant portion that was on data interoperability. Well, I absolutely had no idea what data interoperability even meant. To this day I probably can't explain it very confidently or thoroughly. So, moments before I was to go on stage, that inner anxiety kicked in heavily! As they announced my name to join the others, I was nervous as all get out. As they asked me questions, I answered them from the perspective of the seat in which I sat, based on the information I had at my disposal, and based on what I knew.

After about 25 minutes of in-depth conversation with the three other individuals on the panel—two of whom were doctors, mind

you—we gave our thanks, said our goodbyes, and left the stage.
I exited with a mass of nervous sweat underneath my blazer. I'm not
sure if this was anybody else's story, but that was certainly mine. As
I headed back to my office, which was only a few blocks down the
road, I reflected on what a complete disaster I felt like. I also felt a
little silly because, while I spend a significant amount of my time
speaking in front of people in any number of situations and events, a
part of me felt like I didn't prepare properly. So after toiling over it for
a few hours and having some good chuckles with people in the office,
I mentally moved on. Then, two days later, the link came out saying
that I had access to view the video of the panel.

Here we go again. That sting of the realization about what felt
like a failed panel opportunity focused on data interoperability was
back at the forefront again. As I clicked the link, I thought to myself,
"I'm certain that I'm gonna look absolutely ridiculous on the stage."
To my surprise, as I was listening to how I approached the questions
and to my answers, I realized that I actually fit right in. I wasn't trying
to be someone I wasn't, I wasn't trying to pretend like I knew things
I didn't, and I answered the questions asked of me based on the
information I had, the stakeholder I was representing, and the role
I held at this organization.

As I think back on that experience, I definitely have to point to
one word that sums up how I felt about it all: discomfort. I was
uncomfortable being a part of this topic. I was uncomfortable being
asked certain questions, and I was uncomfortable thinking about how
I would be perceived. Although I truly have no interest in talking
about data interoperability again, I will say that the experience
unlocked a level of confidence and allowed me to see how I can
maneuver in situations where I'm not the expert on a topic but still
have a certain perspective based on the areas in which I do have
expertise.

There are conversations going on around you each and every day. Some of them you feel good about jumping into and giving your insight and some of them you decide to stay away from because you feel like maybe you only have 5% of the knowledge of all the other people around you. Well, do you know how you get additional knowledge and additional confidence to have those conversations? You have to be a part of them. You have to insert yourself in them, in a respectable way of course. And, most importantly, you have to be okay with discomfort, many times. The upside is that the discomfort doesn't last forever.

Once you gain more confidence, become more knowledgeable, and continue to show up at the table and into these conversations, you become even more comfortable and more and more confident. But first you have to show up, even if—especially if—it's uncomfortable.

The next time you're asked to be a part of a meeting or to give your insight based on a topic that you feel like you know 20% of what everyone else in the group knows, don't just bow out of the conversation. Give your perspective based on what you know and on your experiences and grow from there. You may even say, "Based on my experience and my time in the space, my perspective is . . ."

Outside the Workplace

Embracing discomfort for the sake of growth outside of the workplace requires a bit more work. Within the workplace there is lots of track-like behavior, meaning that once you have a role in your workplace, there is opportunity for you to come in and do your particular job, and then go home. So you have this routine where you can just stay in your lane each and every day. In the workplace, we might be forced into discomfort because of a change in our job description, where our office is located, or because of a colleague who is leaving. But, because there's a completely different set of activities happening literally just one cubicle over from you, you can easily get yourself in an area of discomfort for the sake of your learning and growing.

In our personal lives, that becomes a little bit more difficult. It's not difficult because there aren't uncomfortable situations for us to be a part of. It becomes more difficult because it requires us to work harder at being uncomfortable. Because, truly, we really could leave our workplace, take the same route home, eat the same food, serve the same meals, wear the same types of clothes, over and over and over again because it's our choice. In our personal lives, it's our responsibility to make ourselves uncomfortable for the sake of growing in our leadership journey. Whether you decide to volunteer at a new place or lead your next fitness class or even create the next book club opportunity, that's something you have to choose on your own. Although embracing discomfort and new things outside the workplace can technically be more accessible, that shift in us making the decision to do it can sometimes be harder.

But we can do hard things. We do hard things all the time. The next time you're feeling stuck or like you're not sure where to go next, or you're not sure how to elevate in your journey, recognize that you have many opportunities right at your disposal every day. You have the opportunity to switch it up and to get uncomfortable for the sake of your greater good by embracing new things, new environments, and new opportunities.

Run Your Own Leadership Race

Whether inside or outside the workplace, there is one golden rule that I ask you to continuously honor—make a commitment to taking *your own* leadership journey.

I was recently perusing LinkedIn, and I couldn't conduct one full scroll without seeing a litany of announcements about people taking on new jobs, new board appointments, and new opportunities. On all of my other social channels, the same things are happening: announcements and opportunities.

I can understand how scrolling through social and viewing your timeline in search of the next new leadership opportunity and not finding anything can be frustrating. Remember, you're not in competition with any of these people. Your leadership journey is yours and yours alone. It's not a race or competition. Doing too much comparison can actually have a detrimental result, because while you're busy looking to either side of you at what other people are doing, you could be missing out on the opportunities that are being served up right in front of you.

New opportunities are around us everywhere. You must pay attention long enough to see where and what they are and embrace your opportunity to grab hold of the options all around you.

12 Building Your Tribe

Your tribe is essential. While this leadership book and other
books, podcasts, articles, and think pieces you'll run across will
provide essential information for you, it won't be enough. You
need a group of people around you who will help keep you on your
leadership journey.

The word "tribe" can be swapped out for many other words,
including crew, clique, accountability squad, partners, and mentors.
Independent of what you call this group of people, they have one
important goal: to make sure that the leadership path you're on is one
that is accomplished, adds value, and ultimately gets done.

Another reason your tribe is so important is one very simple but
impactful word: change. The unknown future chains of events,
environmental factors, the next global pandemic (that we hope never
happens), the new culture of work, and new budding industries will
all be disruptive and cause change. And while higher institutions offer
new courses and degrees, new certifications are created, and
organizations offer training to take these changes head on, these
things aren't always quickly at our fingertips. Because you are
responsible for your leadership journey, it's in your best interest to

have an easily accessible curated solution to get resources, assistance, counsel, and guidance without a lot of red tape, a huge investment, or traveling too far.

That's when your tribe steps in.

The tribe that you select (keyword *select*) should be available to you for counsel and to hold you accountable. You must be intentional about the individuals you select to be a part of your leadership tribe. This group could be very different from your everyday friend circle. Not to take away from the importance of these friends in your life, but I want to highlight that it is not necessarily the job of your long-time closest friends to be both best friends and confidants and also to be a part of your leadership tribe and accountability crew.

Of course, there may be instances where this could be true. You may have hit the intersection jackpot where some of your closest friends are also able to show up in some of your leadership spaces as well. But that's not required. In many cases it's in your best interest to separate these groups to ensure that there isn't what I like to call social and professional creep. This is where you creep too far on one subject while you're trying to focus in another area. Separating the two makes it a lot easier to stay consistent, maintain focus, and hold whatever goal you're trying to achieve in mind.

So what might this leadership tribe look like?

The upside is that it can look like whatever you want it to look like. But there are a few elements that will make this tribe meaningful, worthwhile, and valuable. Let's explore a few things that you should keep in mind as you're building your ideal tribe.

Pick People Who Aren't Just Like You

Everything in your core is going to want to make you pick people just like you. I get it. If you think you're a pretty cool person, then you probably want to be around people like you. But this isn't the time for that. Your goal here is bigger. This is the time for you to stretch your boundaries, get comfortably uncomfortable, and learn new things about yourself while achieving big leadership goals.

When you're trying to make sure that you are creating a well-rounded circle around you, consider these things:

- Engage with someone who might have a rural experience, since all of your experiences have been in the big city (or vice versa).

- Seek out someone who doesn't have the same gender or ethnic background as you.

- If you've chosen a manufacturing and hands-on career choice, select someone who may have corporate experiences and insight.

I understand this may be a challenging exercise to engage in because you may be stuck at just figuring out *how you even break the ice with someone you initially feel like you have no connection with.* The best way to get started here is with even a loose connection you may have with them. Do you both have children, attend the same religious institution, or maybe even work at the same place? Those simple yet real intersections allow you to open the door to a seamless conversation that will hopefully lead to a deeper, more insightful, and meaningful relationship.

Be Consistent with Your Meetings

Not another meeting! When there isn't a meeting in your life that is mandated, it's so easy to blow it off, reschedule it, or ignore it altogether. Your goal should be to get to the point where your tribe and accountability check-ins are mandatory. Part of being intentional about your leadership journey and the tribe supporting you is that there are dedicated times to focus on feedback and moving forward.

These check-ins should become so essential that they aren't optional meetings that might or might not happen—they *will* happen. This level of consistency can be possible when two key things happen:

1. You pick the people who are going to be just as serious about these meetings as you are.

2. There is a consistent meeting day and time that is only adjusted if it is absolutely necessary.

Pick People Who Aren't Afraid to Disagree with You

Tribe and accountability meetings aren't designed to be high school popularity meet-ups. This is serious business that requires people to be honest, transparent, and forthcoming with what they have to say and the feedback they have to give you. If you're only selecting people who will say *nice* things and who are in 100% agreement with you every time, you're doing yourself a disservice. I mean, what's the point of curating this intentional accountability group to challenge you and help you level up if all you get is praise and accolades? This doesn't challenge you to elevate. Pick people who are committed to giving you good, sound, quality feedback that may be direct and counter to what you want to hear but will ultimately help you unlock and refine your inner leader.

Pick Consistent, Reliable People

I get it—you're busy, I'm busy and so is the rest of the world! But, ironically, we magically show up for the things we care about and commit to.

Imagine for a moment that you're about to go on your dream vacation. It's a place that you've been wanting to visit forever, but you just never prioritized the time or set aside the money to make it happen. Now, finally, it's time. As you work with your travel agent, you discover that the only time that you can make this work is if you leave on a 5:30 a.m. flight. Morning person or not, a 5:30 a.m. flight is *early*!

So, finally, vacation day rolls around and it's time for you to get up. Even if you're not a morning person, you pop up like a rooster on his first day of cockle-doodle-dooing. You're out the door and at the airport with enough time to get through security and board your flight with unexpected energy. All because you're headed on your dream vacation.

Bottom line: we make time for and prioritize the things that we really want to do. Make sure you identify people who are reliable and consistent and actually want to be in your tribe. When times get less than favorable and you need someone to show up for you, you want to know that reliable, trustworthy, and consistent people will be there to support you.

As you're building your tribe, recognize that you are a part of that tribe as well. Just because you're building it for you and you are the focal point, that doesn't mean that you don't have a place and a commitment to give also.

Leadership Tip: Be the leader who doesn't fall into the trap of keeping score. Just because you may have done something for someone in your tribe doesn't mean they have to go out and conduct the same type of favor for you that may cost the same amount of money or take the same amount of time. We all have different needs in our life and on our leadership journey. Commit to being open to receiving what it is that you need while also being a resource to support the journey others are on as well.

When building a tribe, keep this notion of a relationship formula in mind. The relationship formula is a very simple equation that is focused on ensuring that you are both giving and receiving in your relationships.

Deposits and Withdrawals

While most of us want to get something out of our relationships—whether it's love, respect, monetary gain, or a sense of community—it's essential you never let your relationship balance go into the negative. The only way to do this is to give (make deposits) and also receive (make withdrawals). Here are a few ways this formula can serve you:

- It can help change your perspective. We all bring our personal biases, insights, and perspectives to each conversation and situation. It's difficult to fully assess a situation without considering the thoughts and insights of others and how our actions can impact them. By considering the thoughts and perspectives of others, we're able to make more informed and thoughtful decisions.

- It can help increase your bandwidth. While you may have the best intentions of doing everything by yourself, your ever-accumulating obligations may say otherwise. Solid relationships with others allow you to delegate and solicit assistance whenever you need it.

- It can help you navigate diverse personalities. Each of us has our own unique personality and preferences, which can be confusing, complicated, and difficult. By committing to consistently developing your relationships, you have the opportunity to learn how to engage with people and their varying personalities more effectively.

The practice of giving and receiving in a relationship will afford you the opportunity to be of service to people within your circles, while simultaneously shedding the feeling and potential of being only a selfish taker.

As you're curating your tribe, keep in mind those individuals who don't just want to receive things from you, but give as well. In addition to having your own tribe, you may very well be part of others' tribes.

III The Pitfalls

Even with all the leadership material in this book and with all of the other resources that exist, there are still potential pitfalls and traps you can easily slip into. Let's spend some time exploring these areas so that all of your good work isn't mistakenly uprooted.

13 Self-Sabotage

Now, wouldn't it be something if we spent 12 chapters together, you built up an immense amount of confidence, and you're feeling all good about what you're about to do next and then you start doing the unthinkable? It would be quite a shame if, after all this time and the investment you made in your leadership journey, it all came crumbling down based on some actions that you took.

Well, it happens all the time. We are all prone to self-sabotage, which is when we engage in behavior that goes against our wider goals and values. Self-sabotage isn't something that's always intentionally done. It actually happens word by word, phrase by phrase, and situation by situation, often unknowingly.

My job in this chapter, and quite frankly my role throughout the rest of our relationship together, both in this book and beyond, is not only to provide you with actionable leadership tips, tools, and resources but also to ensure that you are doing your part to self-monitor and not self-sabotage. I don't want you to unwind all of the good work you've done to become (more) confident and to be proficient at your current level of leadership and move to your next level.

Before we take action on learning how to recognize self-sabotage and how to avoid it, let's first understand why it happens to us.

Imagine you recently worked on a high-visibility project and you did all the things you needed to do as a leader. You led impeccably, you let others' light shine bright alongside yours, you delegated appropriately, you stayed within the allotted budget, and you delivered more than what you committed to before the deadline. So, when the conclusion of the project came and the accolades began to pour in, you started to feel *some kind of way*—a bit like you didn't deserve being recognized for what was clearly a job well done. Although the accomplishments are clear and the outcomes can't be refuted and the leader of this work—you—is evident, you feel undeserving of this recognition and a bit like a fraud.

When you witness these types of behaviors happening or any behavior that you know isn't ultimately what you need or want to be entrenched in, I always recommend that you name it, *immediately*.

You might recognize right away that you've done good work and recognition is happening, and yet you're having a feeling that is counter to what is normal. You may inwardly say, "I sense self-sabotage" creeping in, and that's good. But know that self-sabotage shows up under the cover of different words and guises, like these:

- Imposter syndrome
- Low self-worth
- Fraudulent operator

Regardless of the term used to describe the behavior, you have to do something about it. Let's explore some ways that self-sabotage often creeps in so you can be aware of it, and either avoid it or quickly recognize it's happening and maneuver out of it.

Using Derailing Phrases

Words matter. We tend to focus a lot on the words other people say to us, when in fact the words we continuously tell ourselves are far more powerful. While we can walk away from others, silence social media, and turn off our streaming devices, we can't walk away from our mind or our mouth. But we can do our part to control what we say and how we think about certain things. The best way to do this is to mind our word choice.

These phrases are examples of self-sabotage:

- "I'll try."
- "Maybe."
- "They're smarter than me, so . . ."
- "I really didn't do that much." (And in actuality, you did.)

In alignment with the principles and lessons of Chapter 9, "Using Your Voice," I also want you to monitor that voice especially when it comes to self-sabotaging words, phrases, and responses that erode your leadership progress. Check yourself when you use them and turn them into positive words reflective of your achievements.

Avoiding the Spotlight

Many people classify themselves as introverts and would rather quietly do their work or handle their commitments and go about their business, and that's okay. I would, however, like to take this moment to advocate not for people to stand in the spotlight solely for themselves (especially if that's not your thing), but for the benefit of others. It is only possible for some people to understand and recognize what they could accomplish by seeing the efforts of someone else.

You are (often unknowingly) a beacon of hope and possibilities, and an example of what could be for someone else.

While I am not someone who shies away from the spotlight, I can remember one distinct moment in my life where I did avoid the spotlight and I do carry some level of regret in doing so. In my mid-20s I graduated with a master's degree in instructional technology with an emphasis on performance improvement and interactive technologies. For some reason I chose not to formally walk in the graduation ceremony to commemorate this accomplishment.

By not participating in this public display, the younger children in my family and some friends were robbed of the opportunity to see what could be possible for them, if they had the same or similar aspiration. Sometimes you are the beacon of possibilities that someone around you needs. You don't have to live in the spotlight, but temporarily stepping into it is just what your inner leader and the leaders watching need.

Prioritizing Everything Except Your Leadership Development

You're busy—I get it. But since everyone is constantly professing to be so busy, I can't help but dig a bit deeper into why this is. How is it that we're always so time impoverished? Is it that we're just so highly sought after every day and people are banging down our door to get time with us? Or might it actually be something different?

Instead of assuming the role of victim, where we think someone is doing something to us, placing something on us, or forcing us to do something, there is a more effective approach. There will always be another commitment, another obligation, another meeting, another phone call, or another text message to write or respond to. If you continuously *allow* your schedule to be filled up and consumed with things that may not be your highest priority or in the best interest of what you want for your future, other people will continue to ask you to do those things and continue to take up your time. There is power and strength in just saying, "No."

Instead, with the things that are a true priority, we put guardrails in place to ensure that they actually happen and we have the time to devote to them. This leadership journey you are on requires focus and prioritization. While yes, we have other commitments in our lives outside of our professional and personal leadership development, the only way that we progress is by identifying the place where we have gaps and prioritizing our elevation.

Believing That Someone Else Is Responsible for Your Leadership Journey

This particular area of self-sabotage is tricky.

On your life journey, you may have experienced a number of leadership and development training scenarios and resources that were provided by an educational institution or at your workplace. And kudos to these organizations for providing this. But here's the truth. The fact that these institutions provided leadership development opportunities needs to be accepted as an additive and supplement to the commitment you have made to lead your journey. Yes, you should take advantage of training and development webinars and educational opportunities, but they should be a part of the leadership plan that you own, manage, and execute. And this journey doesn't end at one job. It continues throughout your career and personal life and weaves through all of your experiences.

Diminishing Your Experience

While I explored some self-sabotage verbiage earlier that has the tendency to water down your words and diminish your overall leadership efforts, you could also be doing yourself a disservice by diminishing your experience in how you present it to others. Take a moment to document a few things:

- How long have you been in your industry?
- How many years of formal education do you have?
- How many professional certifications do you have?
- How many hours have you racked up this year working in your industry?
- How many projects have you successfully led in your area of expertise in the past five years?
- How many projects have you contributed to in the past five years?

While there are many more questions we could explore and gather even more data about your experience, I want you to embrace that you have some, likely a lot. Over time when we've become proficient at doing something, it becomes second nature and perhaps even easy to do it. The fact that it is something you do with ease doesn't mean that it isn't impressive or worth being acknowledged. The next time someone recognizes you for a job well done or even just acknowledges your contributions, avoid these statements:

- "Oh, it was nothing."
- "That didn't take me much time at all."
- "I do this all the time."

The correct response is a lot simpler than that. It only requires you to say, "Thank you."

I'm not suggesting you only take on easy tasks that you know how to do without thinking very hard about them. What I am saying is that the work that you've put in all these years through investing time and money into your formal education, acquiring new certifications, working on new professional projects, making yourself comfortably uncomfortable in social settings, and going above and beyond to become more proficient in your field is in large part why you've become good at it. And because of this, being passive about receiving recognition for wins associated with these accomplishments isn't a value add for you.

Avoid diminishing your experience because it will ultimately give others permission to begin doing the same.

Self-sabotage is a draining and dangerous game. Avoid engaging with it. In the moment of using self-sabotaging language or activities, it may make you feel like you're actually being humble, selfless, and gracious. Instead, you can still do those things with fewer words and in a much more positive, uplifting way—by simply saying, "Thank you."

14 The Leadership Traps

Think about the last time you were sick.

Maybe you had a cold or maybe a serious bout of the flu. Maybe you broke a bone or had to have your tonsils removed or perhaps you even had to have a more serious procedure that involved anesthesia or a stay in the hospital. Whatever it was, I do hope that you've fully healed.

While I know that I'm asking you to reflect back on a not-so pleasant experience, I want you to remember how that experience felt and how often, when you are in this abyss of sickness and being unwell, it's sort of hard to remember what it's like to feel "normal."

Unfortunately in 2021, I had a bout of COVID-19. Although I can fully breathe now and I no longer have a persistent headache and my energy is at high levels, I distinctly remember how challenging it was even just to take a deep breath.

It was truly miserable.

And, as I was quarantining for two weeks, it was really hard to even remember what feeling healthy was like.

Has that ever happened to you? Where you're so deep in the sickly hole that you can't see yourself out or even know what it feels like not to be sick? While most of us don't want to be sick and try to avoid it, it happens and we have to find our way out of it and work hard to regain our energy, our sanity, and our normalcy.

But there are other deep holes we find ourselves in that we have to get out of as well. Do any of these resonate with you?

1. You found yourself in a romantic relationship or friendship that you know isn't serving you or is not of value anymore, but because it's comfortable and what you know, you stay stuck in the trap.

2. You found yourself in a dead-end, unfulfilling career pit stop and although you know you're no longer happy in the position, you can't seem to make the decision to update your resume, refresh your LinkedIn profile, and start networking for a new position, so you stay stuck in the trap.

3. You know that you've picked up a few pounds that you're not happy with and as much as you'd like to (and could) get up off the couch, cut some calories, and start moving your body, you stay stuck in the trap.

Sometimes, even with the best intentions, we find ourselves feeling trapped and helpless in the scenarios of our lives. The ability to fall into, walk right into, or stay stuck in a leadership trap is quite possible as well.

At different points, you may discover that you've said certain things, reacted in particular ways, or made certain decisions that have put you in an unexpected tailspin where you feel stuck, helpless, and trapped. You may start to lose hope and take your eyes off of your goals, forget your abilities, and succumb to just withering away in this trap. In fact, you are really not stuck at all.

You may just feel that way due to embarrassment, burnout, or even a master gut punch to your confidence. Even the stickiest, sharpest, deepest trap can be escaped from, but it requires you to adjust your perspective, accept accountability for where you're at, reframe your approach, and take action.

Before I dive into some of these traps and how to get out of them, I'd like to remind you that many leaders both known and unknown have "fallen from grace" or taken a huge detour from their own leadership tracks and have reemerged as stronger, more astute, more prepared leaders. Some of those leaders include:

Pop Culture and Sports Figures

- Robert Downey Jr.
- Woody Harrelson
- Tim Allen
- Michelle Rodriguez
- Jay Z
- Tiger Woods
- Bruno Mars
- Martha Stewart
- Jacqueline M. Baker (I mean, we know each other now, right?)

Corporate Leaders

- Jamie Dimon, who was fired as president of Citigroup but now is CEO of JPMorgan Chase
- Vanguard founder Jack Bogle, who was removed from his position as president of Wellington Management but then went on to create the index fund and become a leading voice for governance reform

- Steve Heyer, the president of Coca-Cola, who was surprisingly passed over for the CEO position, but then was quickly named head of Starwood Hotels

---

Leadership Tip: Let's not fall into the trap of reading this list of leaders who reinvented themselves and thinking that you're nothing like anyone up there, so the rest of this chapter doesn't apply to you. You can be the leader who finds gems, jewels, and insights in scenarios and in people you may not immediately feel aligned with. With the opening up of this book, you (maybe unknowingly) became the perfect candidate to discover leadership examples, principles, and development opportunities in both unexpected people and unexpected places. To further support this concept, I think about that almost any time I go to a leadership or modern etiquette conference I'm speaking at. As much as I may want to go to a secluded place in the back of the room after I speak to hide out and not be present for another talk, I constantly force myself to stay alert, be visible, and commit to learning something new. And every single time I make this commitment I do just that. Be the leader who doesn't look for ways *not* to learn from other people or other situations. Instead, expect that they'll be there.

While I'm not saying that every leader falls from grace or has a setback and has to claw their way back into the good graces of others, I am saying that we all will make some form of mistake at some point, and recognizing that this will likely happen keeps us from being stuck in our respective traps. It is also prudent to recognize that sometimes because of someone's visibility level (celebrities), we have the tendency to compare and contrast our situation with others as if there is direct alignment. I offered these lists of names as a reference point and not to suggest that what awaits you at some point is a similar leadership snafu where the whole world will witness your leadership hiccup.

Understanding and Escaping the Different Types of Traps

There are traps all around us and I want to be very honest with you in addressing the fact that you can fall prey to them. But you're in luck—once you're in a trap or see yourself heading toward one, there's a way around and out of them. I'll address some of the most common leadership traps along with exploring how to avoid them, and, if you do fall into one, how to emerge from it.

While leadership traps can be vast and plentiful, there are eight major traps that I have seen leaders most commonly fall into during my time in this space:

1. Imposter syndrome

2. Downplaying your abilities

3. Believing there is nothing else to learn or know

4. Forgetting you are a human, not a robot

5. Doing the same thing repeatedly and expecting a different result

6. Hoarding all the tasks

7. Being too busy to cultivate new relationships

8. Not embracing or giving feedback

Let's take a closer look at each trap and ways to avoid them or escape from them.

Imposter Syndrome

You have already run into this term earlier in the book. I cannot help but bring it up again because it continues to be one of the most common traps someone faces as they try to elevate in their leadership journey. Imposter syndrome makes you feel like you are operating fraudulently—like the success or opportunities in front of you are somehow not valid; you are undeserving or not worthy of them. Up to 82% of people manage imposter syndrome. With such a high number of people facing this leadership trap, I tend to double down on it, so that if and when you see it being a part of your world, you know how to manage it. You must be so careful not to fall in this trap because if you start to exude the behavior and mannerisms that you are not deserving of something, very soon other people may pick up on this and begin treating you and your opportunities as undeserving as well. The phrase "you are who you say you are" has weight, has meaning, and can be incredibly impactful. When you feel yourself succumbing to this self-doubt, revisit your Life Thesis. This will allow you to quickly see where you shine bright, and more importantly who you want to be and how you want to be perceived.

Escape from imposter syndrome: Asking yourself key questions helps to silence the inner doubt and to approach things rationally, versus emotionally: Am I qualified to be in this situation? Do I have the right to be in this situation? Do I add value?

Downplaying Your Abilities

Similar to but not the same as imposter syndrome, downplaying your abilities is a direct reflection of experiencing self-doubt. This is especially relevant if the abilities you are doubting that you have are ones that you've in fact demonstrated before. I implore you not to confuse being confident about your abilities with the behavior of being cocky, gloating, or arrogant. Downplaying your abilities is akin to self-sabotage.

Escape from the trap of downplaying your abilities: Think about your abilities and analyze them through a lens of facts. Ask yourself, "Is it a fact that I am competent and capable of this task?" or "Is it factual that I have been successful already in accomplishing these types of things using skills that I have?" By approaching this trap from a factual standpoint, you can minimize the potential emotion that plays into assessing this and speak clearly from a place of truth. It will be necessary for you to be mindful of your word choices in an exercise such as this, but by leaning in to the facts, you are able to be less caught up in fearing that your abilities are connotations of arrogance, but instead valuable skills that you use as a leader.

Believing There's Nothing Else to Learn or Know

Have you ever gone to a class, a conference, or a workshop that started out with information you already felt like you had mastered? I know I have. Honestly, it is painful for me to imagine that I'm about to waste the next 45–90 minutes hearing about a topic that I feel like I already know a lot about. Well, when I honestly think back to those sessions and about what I picked up throughout that time, there has always been something new. Even though my first thought was to find some way to get out of the event based on the agenda or content, I usually have a mental conversation with myself just to calm down and be patient.

Escape from the trap of believing there is nothing else to learn: While it is comforting to be smart and to be filled with knowledge, our ability to learn new things and to be perpetually enlightened also allows us to escape something else—boredom.

Even if I think I'm familiar with all the content and learnings that are presented, my value received from that session could come in other ways, including:

- Understanding someone else's perspective
- Observing how the instructor/presenter presents a concept or topic
- Connecting and networking with others who are interested in the same things

Also, it is in our best interest not to fall into the trap of being a bad listener. As you listen to your colleagues, friends, or even someone you are leading, it is your responsibility to listen and not tune out based on what you think they are going to say. You can miss out on a life-changing moment because you thought that you knew it all. A good leader stays open to listening and learning.

Forgetting We're Humans, Not Robots

Only in the past few years has the world begun fully embracing, recognizing, and acknowledging that we are whole humans. What I mean by this is that as humans, we are more than just our work, more than just our families, and more than just the circumstances that we were born into. We are humans who are filled with accomplishments and career decisions and choices and also humans who have families and feelings and health-related and nonwork-related needs. While it is essential to do what we say we will, be ethical and reliable, it is also essential that we take moments to inquire about more than just work.

Escape the robot life trap: Ask a simple question: "How are you?" Just as important is listening to the answer. This is your first step to evading the "robot lifestyle" trap. You can make a meaningful impact on the lives of the people you are responsible for leading by infusing empathy into your encounters with them. In addition to being empathetic to others as a leader, remember who else you are leading—you. It is your responsibility to recognize when you need to slow down and check in with yourself. You cannot effectively lead anyone else if you are worn down and deenergized. Take moments to recharge, reset, and check in with yourself, so you can be present and impactful for yourself and for others.

Not Embracing Innovation

There is always another level of elevation and perspective to gain. Although we have all amassed a wealth of knowledge and success, none of us have acquired it all, and we never will. To help you gather insight on why this continued mode of elevation and learning is important is directly related to a sneaky 10-letter word that most of us are familiar with. "Innovation" can be such a major contributor in our lives. Our ability to recognize that the world is ever changing and that we have the ability to have an impact on and be in service of these changes is critical. If you think about some of the world's most beloved and impactful brands that either no longer exist or are now less relevant, you'll quickly realize how important it is to stay in a mode of learning, adjusting, and elevating.

Not too far in the past, many of us went into a physical building to secure an item or two or three for entertainment. We knew that we were borrowing this thing and that in a number of days, if we did not return it, we would need to pay a late fee. This place was in the business of providing the new stuff, the old stuff, the funny stuff, the dramatic stuff, the tear-jerking stuff, and the romantic stuff. We remember this place as our local video store and for many of us that was Blockbuster.

While I feel bad sometimes using Blockbuster as an example, it does create a very clear picture of what happens when you refuse to acknowledge that change is always just around the corner. What matters is if we embrace it.

Consider the behemoth that Blockbuster was in its heyday. They steered people to come into a store to select entertainment sources week after week. Although at some point this consumer behavior was predictable and consistent, behaviors changed. This is not a mystery and it happens all the time. The question is *why didn't Blockbuster and other video store chains embrace this and seek to discover other ways to entice, entertain, and meet consumer needs?* With the market share that Blockbuster had, why did they not have a team of R&D staff or product managers who had their eyes on what's next and what could be of future value for customers? Well, that story in itself is a completely different book, but it's a path that they were not on alone.

Several companies (and individuals) have fallen prey to doing the same thing over and over and over again and expecting a different result.

Consider the factory workers who worked the same job loyally for 25 years or more, only to see modern technology innovations eliminate the need for their role. Consider the hairstylist who only did certain styles without embracing new, trendier styles and started to quickly realize that all of their clients moved on to a stylist more in tune with the times.

And, on the scale of Blockbuster, companies like Sears, Kodak, Blackberry, and Xerox have seen similar downfalls because of their inability or unwillingness to take action on the changes of the world and their ability to innovate to meet consumer needs.

Now, there are some companies—legacy companies—that are ensuring they do their part to lean into innovation. From Lego changing the materials of its famous bricks to biodegradable oil-based plastics, to electric vehicles introducing their newest fleets and eliminating the need for engines, innovation is the process of introducing a new idea, method, or device that creates value and solves a pain point or problem. And whether you are representing an organization as a leader or leading yourself, leaning in to innovation and embracing it could be the difference between being relevant or being extinct.

Escape from the trap of not innovating: Many of the examples above had a corporate leaning, but your ability to innovate actually starts with you and on behalf of you. Some people may refer to it as a personal rebrand, a reimagining, or a reintroduction. Well, I'm simply going to call it being flexible and paying attention. The skills you have amassed throughout your life are important and essential for the world that you were in when you acquired them. Since the world is changing—always—we have to "tune up" or check in with our skills to make sure they are relevant to what the world is now. To escape this trap, it is not enough to say, "Well, I know this and this is how it is." As leaders, we must stay aware and willing to learn new things and challenge what we previously learned to ensure that it is relevant to the matter of the current day.

Hoarding All the Tasks Because No One Can "Do It Like You"

Think about something you do incredibly well and do often, perhaps something that you are proud you can do. I want you to be proud of the accomplishment and of anything you have mastered. Now, think for a moment about something else that you want to do—perhaps something that is a life dream or a bucket list item. While the things you have already mastered take up valuable space and time in your life, if you want to do this wish list item, when will you have time to practice, prepare, and ultimately do it? More importantly, might there be another way for this other thing that you mastered to get done?

Escape from the trap of hoarding all the tasks: Create the time and space to acquire new skills by letting go of the things that are not germane to us or that could be more beneficial for someone else to manage. A leader must be able to delegate. While our ego and our pride may guide us into believing only we can do certain things and that our way is the only way, is that really true? Are you really the only person and is your way really the *only* way? I challenge you to think about the skills and things that you want to be good at and embrace that there is time to work on those things if you focus on releasing what you've mastered to someone else so they can elevate to their next level, while you do the same and simultaneously check off the next item on your list.

Being Too Busy to Cultivate New Relationships

We all get the same 168 hours in a week. You don't get more than I do and I don't get more than you. Guess what our beloved role models get? They get the same amount of time as well! And there is always more to do, another conversation to have, or another email waiting to be answered. Because our lives are a continuous onslaught of tasks and commitments and demands, and we have a finite amount of time, it's in our best interest to be very clear about how we are spending this time and who we are spending it with. Embracing new people and new perspectives is in our best interest. When I think about the previous five years of my life, it has not only been my longest years of personal and career elevation, but it has also been the period where I've embraced new friendships, colleagues, and relationships. By getting to know others, you allow yourself to be immersed in new perspectives and even new opportunities. Now, to be very clear, I am not insinuating that your lifelong friendships are to be trashed or that any of these new friendships will rise to the level of a 30-year friendship you deeply value. I want you to acknowledge that, as a leader, you can embrace and cultivate new friendships and new relationships.

Escape from the trap of being too busy for new relationships: I do not doubt for one moment that you are busy. We all are. What I also do not doubt is that you can go your entire life in this state of busyness, filled with regrets and "what ifs" because you were too busy to acknowledge the power you always had to make the time and space for new people and new experiences. In an effort to escape this trap, be mindful of where you are spending your time. Give yourself permission to track exactly where you are spending your weekly 168 hours and once you find an hour or two (because there is always mystery time in our week that we can't seem to pinpoint), take time to cultivate new relationships. You can do this in a number of ways, including:

- Spend some time cultivating your LinkedIn contacts. Are there people within your list you would like to get to know better? Send them a message and set up a quick 15-minute conversation.

- Schedule a 30-minute coffee chat with that new colleague who seems to keep to themselves.

- Spark up a conversation with the person who just joined your new gym who seems to be a loner (perhaps like you). Talk about their gym bag, workout clothes, or yoga mat. Yes, it may seem uncomfortable at first, but sometimes sparking a quick conversation is just as easy as offering a quick, genuine compliment.

- Another approach is to re-spark a relationship that used to be stronger. We've all had friendships and relationships that were much stronger than they are now. If you desire to rebuild that relationship, be the leader who reaches out to reconnect and hopefully infuse some meaning back into the relationship that once was.

We need people and human connection. As some of our legacy relationships age and as we begin to give ourselves permission to try new things, we often need new relationships to support the new decisions that we've made for our lives, our careers, and our families. Be the leader who escapes the *no new friends* mantra and embraces new people, new opportunities, and new experiences.

Not Embracing or Giving Feedback

Have you ever heard someone say, "If I knew then what I know now . . ." It essentially means, if only I had the wisdom, insight, feedback or information that I now know, earlier in my life, I would have potentially done _____ differently. While time travel, mind reading, and shapeshifting are not possible yet (to my knowledge), there is something that is close enough to help us get the insight we need to make better decisions, faster. It's feedback.

As a leader, it is in our best interest to both give and receive quality feedback. The word "quality" here is really essential. It is quite easy to tell someone "good job" or " well done" with no additional context or feedback. You know what's a bit harder? Saying, "Good job, and here are a few places to elevate next time." Providing good-quality, actionable feedback allows you to know that you are setting someone else up for success.

Escape from the trap of not embracing or giving feedback: Some people move in and out of their careers and relationships, making glaring errors and missteps no one ever lets them know about. Year over year, they are never given the feedback that could help them make small but meaningful adjustments that elevate their work or leadership, and are not even aware they are operating ineffectively. Quality feedback would afford them this opportunity to make adjustments and elevate to being a stronger leader. When you find yourself in a place of not wanting to receive or give feedback, just whisper to yourself, "This could be what is needed." Meaning, this one little piece of feedback that you would be giving or receiving could be *the* piece that could elevate them or you or completely resolve the situation.

Being Mindful of Leadership Traps

If you know that you are deep in a place where you have not received feedback for quite some time and you are not even sure how to solicit it, start with people who you know care about you and have your best interest at heart. Since you know at your core that this feedback will come from a place of love, the goal is that you can then move on to gather feedback from other people with whom you may not have as intimate a relationship.

Leadership traps are all around us, but so are the opportunities to avoid and escape them. Be the leader who is committed enough to pursue your next level of leadership and aware enough to look out for traps that may derail or misguide your leadership journey.

You must be careful of the leadership traps. You could easily commit to your leadership journey, land on and create your Life Thesis, and even amass clarity around which leadership styles most resonate with you. But then, in the blink of an eye, you could get perpetually caught up in one of these leadership traps that keep you captive from what your next level could be. Your role as an everyday leader at all of your potential levels is to be mindful that the traps exist. Take time to check in with yourself, consider what is going well and what is not, and what obstacles you have put in your own way that prevent you from moving forward.

It is also necessary for you to acknowledge that getting caught in these traps and even stuck there for a while is not the end for you. I have had to claw my way out of the feedback trap. For years, I went without getting quality feedback and had to relearn what it meant (and felt like) to receive both praise and constructive criticism and do something meaningful with the feedback.

If you find yourself approaching or exhibiting behaviors that will only lead you into a trap, self-correct and step over it. It won't always be easy but it will always be worth it. And if you wake up one day and realize you are already in one of the traps, acknowledge it, use the tips in this chapter to get out of it, and the next time a trap appears, step over it versus stepping in it.

I remember when I got some real time feedback from Jacqueline Welch. The interesting part of this particular feedback is that it wasn't even given in a way that presented itself like feedback. I was ranting about a situation where I thought I had been treated unfairly. After intentionally listening to my complaints without interrupting one time, she just asked me if I had considered a couple of things. Her calm and direct demeanor and questions made me realize that there were some things that I hadn't considered in assessing the situation.

Her feedback, phrased in the form of questions, was effective, clear and, more impactful than if she had gone into an all-out lecture.

So, know that while engaging in feedback sessions is essential, it can often be done not just with statements and phrases but also with questions.

Now is the perfect time for you to consider: *How do you best give and receive feedback?*

15 Leading versus Following

After diving deep into what it means to be a leader, it might seem a little out of place for me to discuss the concept of following, especially as I prepare to close out this book. But it's important to discuss the concept of following as a leader while we're so deep into the book.

Let me explain. There have been several concepts throughout this book that demystify and further define how you should maneuver in your life to be perceived as the best possible leader.

As you do so, it's not always necessary for you to be in the spotlight, to be the center of attention, or to be the most important person or topic of discussion to claim your rightful place as a leader. Within the world of leadership, there is a time to be the main attraction and there is a time to be the co-star. Make sure you are ready to both lead and follow, since doing both is the hallmark of an effective leader.

While I deeply subscribe to the notion that it is your responsibility to declare you are a leader and to utilize the opportunities around you each and every day to elevate to your next level, there is also a way to do that by not playing the main character and instead playing a supportive role.

The very act of understanding when to step aside and when to step up is a pivotal component of your leadership journey. It is a direct reflection of your ability to embrace the various degrees of leadership levels and knowing that as you venture in and out of the levels of leadership, you have the ability to take on different roles.

Within these levels of leadership are the important acts of leading yourself and leading others and institutions and organizations and communities. If you're going to thrive as a leader, it's not going to be necessary or even beneficial for you to be the only person in the lead *all* the time.

When will there ever be space for others to lead? When will there be space for others to rise to their next level? If you're taking up all the oxygen in all the spaces as the key individual in charge every single time, when will your commitment to leading other people be fulfilled? After all, being a leader is just as much about giving others the opportunities to elevate in their own leadership journey.

And, more importantly, as much as it may seem like a magical idea always to be in the spotlight and always on, trust me, it gets old, it gets tired, and at some point your mind and body aren't happy about that.

To bring this leading versus following concept to life, I'll run through some examples. I want to make sure you have a thorough understanding of when it might be time for you to play the main character and when you need to step aside to allow others to lead under your guidance and oversight, and with your support.

But first, let me be the leader who shares one of my biggest lessons in leading versus following.

My Leading versus Following Adventure

I made a very bold decision in 2021 to resign from my corporate position. While I know that people resign from their positions all the time, my particular situation was a bit different.

For 10 years prior to resigning, I had slowly been growing my leadership consultancy, Scarlet Communications. This company, which originally started with a focus on etiquette specifically for teen girls, had a tremendous amount of growth, elevation, and reimagining over those 10 years. Although it started out as an etiquette-focused business, I advanced our focus to a leadership consultancy that teaches etiquette as one of the parts of the leadership journey.

In my corporate role, I led a team of multiple individuals and I took great pride in ensuring these individuals were supported and challenged. I also endeavored to put each in position to elevate to their next level of leadership. When I made the decision to leave, I went through a series of mental and physical exercises to ensure that I was preparing the team for success after I was gone.

In my role as vice president of startup programming at one of the nation's largest nonprofits, one of the core responsibilities my team and I had was discovering some of the best and brightest startups in the fin tech and health tech spaces. We produced large-scale pitch competitions and we also supported other accelerator programs that surfaced and discovered disruptive startups as well.

I quietly made the decision to resign in August 2021 with the intent to make my last day February 25, 2022, exactly eight years to the day of starting at the organization. This gave me a solid six months to personally and mentally prepare and secretly prepare my team.

One of the ways I prepared was by taking a back seat to some of the major productions that my team was responsible for. Honestly, this was difficult for me because of my past life as an event producer. As I've shared previously, I can unintentionally get deeply immersed in the details of a situation because that skill set once served me in a previous career in events. Now that it's not a critically needed skill in my corporate role, I have to remind myself to suppress it.

Luckily—or maybe I should say thankfully—I led and was supported by a team of very talented, committed, and impressive individuals. They understood the power of autonomy, and they knew I would provide them with enough support and room to move forward, lead in their own lanes, and reach back for help if they needed it.

Also, I will add that there were two key things that happened around the time that I had privately made the decision to resign that made this transition more digestible. In August 2021 I contracted COVID-19, which had me on the outs for a while. Then, in mid-September of that year, my father suddenly passed away. Both of these events happened at the most inopportune time (not that there's ever a good time to get COVID or for a loved one to pass away), but the timing really forced the team, and me, to go into full-speed independence mode without me there for oversight. So, even if I had somehow fallen into a trap of being overprotective and not wanting to step aside to allow my team to lead in their lanes, my absence basically forced the situation. This is a good example of how even when you're in a lead role, it will be necessary and often most beneficial for you to step aside and let the team do what they've been observing from you and what you've been hopefully preparing them for. I could have gone the route of being overly protective and attempted to be in on every conversation and every decision point, but that would have made the team incredibly reliant on someone who actually had plans to resign, even though they didn't know it at the time.

So while I must admit that stepping to the side and letting those who you've been leading now lead on their own is often hard, it is very necessary if you want to have the space and the bandwidth to move to your next level, while also equipping those you are leading to do the same.

When the day came that I announced my resignation, there was sadness and there were tears, but there was no apprehension about my team's ability to thrive. They were ready.

The other part of this leading versus following consideration was the onslaught of questions I received as a result of my decision to leave. Here's the thing: I greatly enjoyed my work and my team at the organization. My decision to leave had nothing to do with dissension with the work, the people, or the mission. It was simply a matter of taking the lead on the thing that brings me the most joy, allows me to make the most impact, and creates a world filled with more confident, capable, and inspiring leaders. It was truly a decision of me leading versus following.

So how can you decipher when to lead and when to follow? This table shows some scenarios that will help to shape your thinking around leading versus following and potential approaches to take.

The Scenario	The Potential Approach
You and your team are charged with launching a new product within a year and the team is unfamiliar with this type of launch. You are the formal leader of this team, with all individuals reporting to you.	**Leading:** While there may be components of this project that the team can certainly be responsible for, this scenario calls for a strong leader to direct and steer the team appropriately.

(Continued)

The Scenario	The Potential Approach
You have been running point on a project for three years, with a few colleagues supporting you. You're ready to move on to your next challenge and a colleague is ready to take more of a prime role in this current project.	**Following:** This is the perfect opportunity for you to follow your colleague's lead and support them as you free up bandwidth to move to your next thing.
While you've been leading the family reunion planning for the past 10 years, you've grown uninterested in all of the details necessary to effectively execute it. A much younger family member has expressed interest in taking a bigger role in planning.	**Following:** Since your passion and interest for planning this family reunion has waned, this is an opportunity for you to mentor and support this family member so they have the experience and wisdom to execute this in an effective way.
You've been planning your annual girls' trip for four years. You enjoy it, you have the bandwidth to do so, and your friends enjoy it as well. You have not grown weary of it, and at this point no one has expressed interest in co-planning or completely assuming the responsibilities of planning.	**Leading:** While there are always possibilities for you to grow and elevate, if you are in a situation that you enjoy and that you consider fulfilling and of value to you, feel free to continue to lead and acquire different skills to help you lead even better. In this situation, while you may be completely happy with being the lead, is there an opportunity for you to further refine your delegation skills by soliciting assistance for one of the planning components that someone else is great at? You still retain your leadership "role" while also directly letting someone else elevate their skills as well.

Think about one of your absolute favorite movies. Mine happens to be *The Thomas Crown Affair*, but think for a moment about what yours is. Imagine that you've watched the movie (again) and the credits have started to roll. The three or four people in the major roles usually appear at the very top of the cast list and then the slew of individuals involved in the entire movie production *follow*. The truth is that while the main characters stand in the bright lights, the movie would not exist if the many individuals listed in the credits were not there doing the work. Furthermore, while the main characters always appear to be in the *lead*, they too are doing a substantial amount of following. If you have ever watched the behind-the-scenes development of any movie, you see that the director is actually the one running the show, leading the next scene, the next fighting sequence, or the dramatic ending.

When you think about watching an actor called on stage to accept an award for their role, they usually go into a sequence of thank-yous. And who are they thanking? Normally, it's the individuals who played the *following* roles and supported the actions of the person publicly receiving the award.

Leadership Tip: It's rare that we arrive on a successful path, solely by the work that we've done on our own. Good leaders at all levels take the time to express gratitude for people who have helped them arrive at a certain place.

Leading is just as important as following. Our ability to be open to assessing when we should be taking on either of these roles is equally important. Also, know that if you are following in a situation, this does not mean you lose your master title of being a leader. Leadership and your ability to be an effective leader is independent of you supporting something as a follower.

A good leader knows that leading effectively is just as important as following.

CONCLUSION

Expect Leadership

We've spent a lot of time focused on the unexpected nature of leadership. I mean, it's literally the title of this book.

Even when the world doesn't see you coming, even when you've been in a situation when you didn't really believe in yourself, and even when you're faced with the most challenging and impossible situation, you have the ability to remind yourself of your leadership abilities, your leadership potential, and your leadership opportunities.

Remember that leadership isn't just for certain types of people or certain career choices. It's not just for people of a certain salary range or people who live in a particular neighborhood. It's not just for the scholarly and higher educated. It's not only for the super social and extra extroverted.

You know who leadership is for?

It's for You!

With imperfections, bouts of anxiety, missteps, mistakes, unpolished and checkered pasts, setbacks, and misdirection, you can still claim the road of leadership and actually expect it!

I'm glad that you've made the commitment to explore this book and immerse yourself in the content, principles, and lessons.

My hope for you is that you walk away from this book inspired, enlightened, and filled with the positive energy to continue elevating in your leadership journey. I also hope that you'll revisit these pages if you stray off track, get knocked out of focus, or just need a little pick-me-up to keep growing.

You are ready.

There's just one thing left to do.

Today, and every day, remember and declare that you are a leader and you're ready to take the journey to discover, define, and refine the leader within you!

Go embrace your inner unexpected leader.

ABOUT THE AUTHOR

Jacqueline M. Baker has a commitment to inspiring people like you and organizations just like yours to take meaningful action. From podcast producer and author to founder and speaker, Jacqueline occupies spaces to help you embrace your inner leader, confidently advance to your next level, and Just Start™ the things you want to do.

Jacqueline founded Scarlet Communications, a global leadership consultancy, in 2012. With thousands of students, Fortune 500s, and community organizations across the globe, Jacqueline makes meaningful impact with a modern, relatable, and digestible approach to leadership content creation and delivery. She evangelizes that leadership isn't just a skill or concept reserved only for those in executive roles, but that we all have the power to lead in our own unique ways across both social and professional settings. Her first book, *Leader by Mistake: Becoming a Leader One Mistake at a Time*, shows how you too can find your inner leader by learning from your mistakes and homing in on the skills you already possess, to lead confidently.

Prior to launching Scarlet, Jacqueline spent nearly a decade in corporate leadership roles for companies like AT&T, Chrysler, Ford Motor Company, and AAA of Michigan. Her most recent corporate role as Vice President of Startup Programming at AARP Innovation Labs provided a unique opportunity to discover disruptive startups across the globe and identify ways to collaborate with one of the nation's largest nonprofits. She also aided in the leadership development of these startup organizations.

Jacqueline also supports leadership opportunities in the corporate governance space as she serves as an independent corporate board member at Plastipak Packaging on the Functional Leadership Development Committee.

Jacqueline holds two degrees from Wayne State University, a bachelor of arts in public relations and a master's of education in instructional technology with specializations in interactive technologies and performance improvement. She is a graduate of the Protocol School of Washington, with a focus on international etiquette and protocol, and holds a Six Sigma Green Belt certification in process improvement, which she uses to help clients develop systems and processes that will allow them to reach their strategic planning and leadership development goals.

Outside of her professional and educational endeavors, she enjoys mentoring both young and seasoned leaders and serving nonprofit organizations like 12 Days DC Metro and the Royal Society of the Arts, traveling, watching James Bond movies, and hitting the slopes during the winter for some snowboarding.

Jacqueline also hosts the podcast *Just Start™: From Ideas to Action*. Every chance she gets, she is an avid dinner party host and loves to convene meaningful groups of people for great conversation, idea sharing, and accountability, paired with delicious cuisine and cocktails. For more about Jacqueline, head over to www .jacquelinembaker.com.

Connect with Jacqueline on social:

Instagram: @magicaljax

LinkedIn: Jacqueline M. Baker

Facebook: Jacqueline M. Baker

INDEX

NOTE: Page numbers in *italics* refer to figures.